ENHANCING
THE ACTIVITIES OF
DAILY LIVING

Laura Town
Karen Kassel
Rachael Mann

Ω
OMEGA
PRESS

Ω Omega Press
Zionsville, IN 46077

Production Credits:
Authors: Laura Town, Karen Kassel, and Rachael Mann
Publisher: Omega Press
Photos: All images used under license from Shutterstock.com

Social media connections:
Laura Town
Twitter: @laurawtown

Karen Kassel
Twitter: @KarenKassel1

Rachael Mann
Twitter: @RachaelLMann1

ENHANCING THE
ACTIVITIES OF DAILY LIVING

Nothing about the Alzheimer's process is easy. One of the more stressful phases for both the individual with Alzheimer's disease and the caregiver is the gradual loss of independence which results from the inability to perform certain tasks. In general, these tasks fall into one of two categories: activities of daily living (ADL) and instrumental activities of daily living (IADL). Broadly defined, ADL are basic self-care tasks necessary for maintaining health and well-being, whereas IADL are more complex tasks essential for independent living.

Not knowing how to drive, how to cook, how to bathe, or even how to use the toilet is frightening for both you and your loved one. Over time, your loved one may forget how to perform both ADL and IADL, which will increase their need for a full-time caregiver. This lack of independence places an incredible stress and strain on caregivers. What makes this process more confusing is that at the beginning, individuals might remember how to complete tasks on some days and not others. In my (Laura's) father's case, he sometimes knew when to use the toilet and other times did not. When he realized that he was becoming incontinent, it added to his depression and he seemed to decline at a faster rate than he previously had. As a caregiver, you must assess whether your loved one needs help with certain tasks and what degree of assistance is required. You also need to understand techniques you can use to help your loved one complete these tasks while retaining as much independence as possible.

In addition, as the disease progresses you may notice your loved one exhibiting behaviors that are uncharacteristic for their personality. These may range from simply saying things that seem odd or inappropriate to acting in ways that could be dangerous to you, your loved one, or others. Being prepared for these changes and knowing how to respond to them is crucial.

The checklists in this book will provide you with information you may need to help your loved one perform essential activities and face behavioral challenges. This information is particularly important if you are a live-in caregiver or provide at-home care for your loved one. As you review this information, remember that every individual with Alzheimer's disease has different strengths and difficulties. As such, the suggestions throughout this book can and should be tailored to fit your loved one's specific needs.

Activities of Daily Living

Activities of daily living, or ADL, include care and hygiene activities that must be completed in the course of a typical day. In general, the tasks involved in ADL are learned early in life and include things such as taking a bath, getting dressed, and brushing teeth. Activities related to eating, communicating, and moving around are also considered ADL.

Small declines in the ability to perform ADL—such as missing a bath or wearing a day-old shirt—may pose no imminent danger to your loved one. If left unchecked, however, ADL declines can lead to illness, infection, and other serious health issues. As a caregiver, you must recognize where potential needs exist and be prepared to offer supportive, low-pressure assistance to your loved one. The following checklist discusses tips for helping your loved one perform ADL.

Checklist: *General tips for helping your loved one perform ADL*

☑ When helping with ADL, involve your loved one as much as possible. If you start taking over activities, your loved one will forget how to do them on their own much more quickly.

☑ Offer help as tactfully and compassionately as possible. Treat your loved one with dignity at all times. Your attitude as a caregiver will be reflected in your loved one's actions.

☑ Give directions one step at a time.

☑ Stick to a routine as much as possible. Consistency and routine will help your loved one be more compliant when asked to perform ADL.

☑ If your loved one becomes defiant or aggressive, don't force them. Let them have their way, and come back to it later. They may forget that they didn't want to perform the task just a few hours earlier.

☑ Consider reasons your loved one may resist performing ADL (e.g., lack of privacy when taking a bath), and try different methods to work around their reluctance. Strategies that work for one individual may not work for another. Determine what works best for your loved one.

☑ Remember that many tasks seem stressful, frustrating, and confusing for individuals with Alzheimer's disease. Therefore, your loved one faces a series of difficult tasks all day long. This may lead to exhaustion and defiance when asked to perform the next task, especially if they have forgotten the importance of the task. Be patient and positive throughout each task, and provide a lot of encouragement.

☑ If you are getting frustrated with your loved one and your loved one can be safely left alone for a few minutes, walk away from the situation and take some time to refocus and calm yourself. You might want to use this time to consider other strategies for helping your loved one. When you regain a sense of peace, go back to helping your loved one with the task they were trying to complete.

☑ Be realistic about what your loved one can do given their current level of impairment. Focus on your loved one's remaining abilities instead of dwelling on their lost abilities.

☑ Don't constantly remind your loved one of their problems with ADL. This only serves to embarrass them in the moment, and they won't remember your admonishment or directions the next time anyway.

☑ If your loved one is engaging in a repetitive behavior that is not harmful (e.g., tearing tissues, wiping the counter), let them do it. This may soothe their nerves.

☑ Be consistent. If you say you will do something, follow through.

☑ Remember that your loved one's inability or refusal to perform ADL is because of their disease, not their personality. Understanding your loved one's disease and their particular needs and fears can help you discover ways to work around your loved one's reluctance or inability to perform ADL.

Bathing

Bathing is a particularly challenging ADL for individuals with Alzheimer's disease and their caregivers. Your loved one may forget that they need to bathe or view it as unpleasant because they must disrobe. They may also develop a fear of water.

From a safety standpoint, bathing presents many potential hazards for individuals with Alzheimer's disease, including slipping, drowning, and electrocution. Therefore, helping your loved one bathe as the disease progresses is an important caregiving task. The questions below can help you determine whether your loved one needs help bathing.

Checklist: *Assessing whether your loved one needs help bathing*

☑ Does your loved one forget that they need to bathe?

☑ Does your loved one get defensive when you ask whether they've bathed?

☑ Does your loved one use scalding or cold water instead of warm water to bathe?

☑ Is your loved one afraid of water or afraid of falling?

☑ Has your loved one had a previous bad experience with bathing (e.g., slipped or got burned by water that was too hot)?

☑ Does your loved one have a medical condition or take medication that may increase their risk of dizziness, lightheadedness, or disorientation? This would put them at increased risk for falling in the bath.

☑ Has your loved one forgotten the sequence of steps for bathing?

☑ Does your loved one complain about being too hot or too cold in the bathroom?

☑ Does your loved one often forget why they entered a room?

☑ Is your loved one afraid of being left alone?

☑ Has your loved one lost their sense of smell? This may contribute to not recognizing body odor.

Once you have determined that your loved one needs help bathing, you must figure out the best methods for offering assistance. In doing so, you must consider your loved one's hygiene and safety needs as well as their desire for independence. This can be a delicate balance and will require some trial-and-error and creative thinking on your part. The tips below will help you create a safe bathing environment for your loved one and develop a routine that is acceptable to them. A more

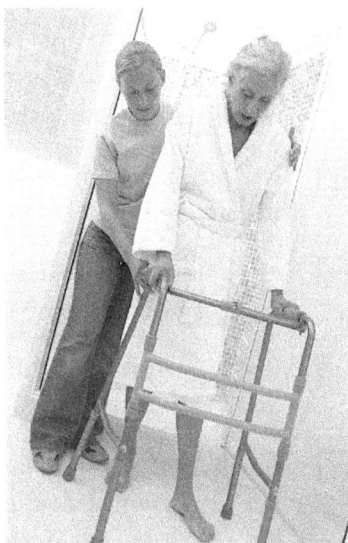

Credit: JPC-PROD

complete discussion about safety is included in *Home Safety Checklist Guide and Caregiver Resources for Medication Safety, Driving, and Wandering.*

Checklist: *Bathing safety*

☑ Add nonslip decals to the bottom of the tub.

☑ Install a shower rail and an anchored bench seat.

☑ Adhere bath rugs to the floor to prevent slipping.

☑ Use colored mats and rugs inside and outside the tub to help your loved one judge water depth and be able to focus.

☑ Don't use bath oils, which can make bath surfaces slippery.

☑ Eliminate unnecessary toiletries in the bathroom and shower. Your loved one may become confused and use products incorrectly.

☑ Keep soap, shampoo, towels, and washcloths within easy reach to avoid leaning and falling.

☑ Keep electronics away from the tub or shower, especially electric razors, hairdryers, and curling irons.

☑ Keep cleaning products and other unnecessary hazardous items locked away from your loved one.

☑ Use or install a walk-in shower or tub if possible so your loved one can avoid having to climb over the side of the tub.

☑ Replace glass sliding doors on the tub or shower with plastic doors or a shower curtain.

☑ Install handles instead of knobs for the water faucet. Handles provide a more obvious clue than knobs of how far the water line is open.

☑ Remove the bathroom door lock so your loved one does not get locked in the bathroom, either intentionally or unintentionally.

☑ If your loved one needs help bathing, do not leave them unattended in the bath area.

☑ Test the water temperature before allowing your loved one into the bath. This is primarily to prevent scalding, but it also can prevent chills. You may want to purchase a heat sensor that changes color when the water is too hot.

☑ Use safe lifting techniques so you don't strain your back while helping lift or steady your loved one.

☑ Use a shampoo that will not sting if it gets in your loved one's eyes.

☑ Use liquid soap instead of bar soap that your loved one may slip on.

☑ Elderly people often have fragile skin. To avoid breaking the skin, rub gently rather than scrubbing. Also make sure the water pressure is not too hard. Pat the skin dry rather than rubbing.

☑ Seat your loved one while drying them off or changing their clothes to prevent falling.

☑ Dry up puddles of water immediately.

☑ Although maintaining a warm room is important to avoid chills, avoid space heaters that may cause a fire, burn, or electrocution hazard.

Checklist: *How to help your loved one bathe*

☑ Set a schedule for when your loved one should bathe, and bathe at the same time of day every day. If your loved one had a routine before they developed Alzheimer's disease, stick with that routine unless circumstances require a change (e.g., nighttime incontinence or sundowning).

☑ Use a consistent routine for bathing. If you find one method that works well, use it every time your loved one needs to bathe. If over time this routine begins to not work well, establish a new routine that does work.

☑ Involve your loved one with the decisions. Ask if they prefer a bath or a shower, which soap or towel they want to use, etc. Provide only two options for each decision.

☑ Instead of asking your loved one if they want to bathe, tell them that their bath or shower is ready. Mention how much they enjoy taking a bath or shower.

☑ Have everything ready before leading your loved one to the bath, because if you leave to get something they may abandon the idea of taking a bath.

☑ Make sure your loved one uses the toilet before bathing to avoid accidents in the bath.

☑ Make sure the bathroom is well lit.

☑ Keep the room and water warm to prevent your loved one from getting chilled.

☑ Demonstrate how warm and soothing the water is by scooping some water from the bath into your loved one's hand.

☑ Use as little water as necessary in the bath, especially if your loved one is afraid of entering the water or afraid of deep water. Two to three inches of water is adequate for a bath.

☑ Use distractions to keep your loved one's mind off the bath, such as listening to music or talking about a favorite subject.

☑ Simplify the bathing steps. Use a combination shampoo/conditioner, or separate the bathing steps from washing their hair. Other useful products may include dry shampoo, no-rinse soap, or combination shampoo/soap.

☑ Give your loved one a washcloth, bath mitt, or other colorful item to occupy their hands.

☑ As you bathe your loved one, explain to them what you are doing and why. Remember to speak slowly, and don't be afraid to repeat yourself if your loved one seems confused.

☑ Warn your loved one what the next step is before you do it. For example, say "I'm going to wash your arm now."

☑ If your loved one is still capable of performing the bathing steps, give them one instruction at a time to follow. Encourage your loved one to help as much as possible.

☑ Use both verbal instructions and nonverbal demonstrations to show your loved one how to bathe.

☑ To rinse the hair or body, use a hand-held sprayer or a pitcher with water.

☑ Be sure to cleanse (and dry) hard-to-reach areas such as under skin folds, under the breasts, and the genital area. The genital area is especially important to clean daily if your loved one has a problem with incontinence.

☑ Use a sponge bath with no-rinse soap to clean your loved one on days they do not take a bath. You can wrap them in a large towel and give them a "massage" to help you be successful in cleaning them.

☑ Do not rush the bath, as this may agitate your loved one.

☑ Use a terrycloth robe rather than a towel to dry your loved one if they are impatient. If needed, use cornstarch powder to absorb excess moisture from skin folds.

☑ Always praise and compliment your loved one's efforts after the bath is complete. Do not focus on things that don't go well.

Another important consideration when assisting your loved one with bathing is their desire to maintain a sense of modesty. Individuals with Alzheimer's disease may find the experience of disrobing in front of others unpleasant and frightening, which can increase resistance to bathing. The following checklist offers some ideas for helping your loved one maintain their privacy.

Checklist: *How to give your loved one privacy*

☑ Be sensitive to the fact that most older adults have a sense of modesty and will resist undressing in front of someone. This is normal.

☑ Allow a caregiver of the same gender to help with the bath.

☑ Avoid making your loved one walk from the bedroom to the bathroom, or vice versa, naked or with only a small towel wrapped around them. Give them an ample robe and allow them to disrobe, undress, or dress in the bathroom.

☑ Keep the bathroom door closed and windows covered for privacy while your loved one is bathing.

☑ Use distraction techniques to keep your loved one's mind off the fact that they are naked. Sing a song, tell a story, or make conversation. Humor is also a good way to distract your loved one and make them feel less awkward.

☑ If your loved one mentions that they don't like other people watching, cover the mirror so they don't see their (or your) reflection.

☑ If your loved one is comfortable with deeper water, add bubble bath to the water and allow the bubbles to provide some privacy.

☑ If your loved one is able to perform bathing tasks on their own, provide limited assistance such as handing them the soap and washcloth and then turning away while they wash.

☑ If your loved one can follow simple directions, allow them to do the actual bathing while you provide simple, step-by-step instructions, such as telling them to wash their arm, wash their leg, etc.

☑ Uncover and wash only one part of the body at a time. By the end of the bath, your loved one may forget their objection to being naked.

☑ Be respectful and matter-of-fact about cleaning genitalia. Offer your loved one a warm washcloth and prompt them to clean their own genitalia. If they refuse or can't wash on their own, clean the area gently while making distracting conversation. Be sure to check for lesions or rashes while washing if you can.

☑ Avoid focusing your eyes on your loved one's private parts for long periods of time.

☑ Cover your loved one's private parts with a washcloth in the tub to provide some privacy, or allow your loved one to wear a light robe in the tub. This may be cumbersome, but it may help them feel more comfortable accepting help.

☑ Allow your loved one to dry off on their own if they are physically capable. While they are dressing, surreptitiously check for damp spots and quickly dry them with a small towel.

☑ Lay out clothing before the bath so that your loved one can quickly go from drying to dressing to reduce the amount of time they are naked.

☑ If your loved one refuses to let you help them bathe, consider hiring a home services agency to provide help. Your loved one may be more willing to let a stranger help them than someone they know.

Sometimes, your loved one will resist or refuse bathing despite your best efforts to provide a safe, private environment in which to do so. When this occurs, remain patient and upbeat, and consider the tips in the checklist below.

Checklist: *What do I do if my loved one refuses to bathe?*

☑ If your loved one refuses to bathe after several minutes of persuasion, drop the subject and come back to it later.

☑ If your loved one refuses to bathe, use situations such as going out or having company to give them a reason to bathe.

☑ Never force your loved one into the tub or shower. This may instigate defiance, aggression, or panic.

☑ If the bathroom has busy wallpaper, remove it or paint over it with a solid color. Busy patterns may agitate your loved one and prevent them from voluntarily entering the bathroom.

☑ Remove all clutter from the bathroom, including decorations and hygiene items. Store hygiene items in drawers or cabinets to keep them out of sight. Clutter may disorient your loved one and make them want to avoid the bathroom.

☑ Start preparations and guide your loved one to the tub or shower without mentioning a bath.

☑ If the noise of running water scares your loved one, run the bath water before they enter the room, and avoid showers.

☑ If your loved one is frightened of entering the water but doesn't mind running water, fill the tub with water after your loved one is in the tub.

☑ Make sure you provide adequate privacy for your loved one in the bathroom.

☑ If your loved one is afraid of deep water, set up a bath seat for them to use. Pad the seat for comfort.

☑ If an overhead shower is frightening for your loved one, consider installing a handheld shower.

☑ If you are a spouse or a same-gender adult child, consider joining your loved one in the shower. Doing so may lessen your loved one's objections when they see the process is safe and normal for someone else.

☑ If your loved one regularly dyed their hair in the past, tell them you are dying their hair and they must remain in the shower to wash their hair for several minutes.

☑ If your loved one states that they've already taken a bath even though they haven't, keep a record of baths and show it to them as proof that they haven't bathed that day. The same technique can be used if your loved one takes several baths each day and states that they haven't yet taken a bath.

☑ Record on a year-long calendar when your loved one takes their baths. After a while, you can use the calendar as proof that taking a bath on a certain day of the week is normal.

☑ Have your loved one's physician write an order to take a bath on a prescription pad and show it to your loved one as proof that they need to take a bath. Have the doctor write several "prescriptions" in case your loved one tears them up.

☑ Make bath time fun by connecting it with enjoyable activities before and after the bath.

☑ Try giving your loved one a full bath or shower twice a week and giving them a sponge bath with no-rinse soap or a quick cleanse of the face and genitals on other days. A sponge bath can also be useful if your loved one is afraid of the water.

Dressing

Dressing is another ADL that can prove difficult and frustrating for individuals with Alzheimer's disease as the disease progresses. The process can become overwhelming because of the choices it presents. For example, your loved one may not understand the seasons anymore, so they may choose to wear shorts in the winter or heavy clothes in the summer. It also becomes physically difficult to dress as your loved one loses the dexterity needed to manage buttons and zippers. In addition, your loved one may forget the purpose of these fasteners or the order in which they are supposed to put on their clothes. In the later stages of the disease, your loved one may also forget how to move their arms and legs in order to get them through the appropriate holes.

As a result of these factors, your loved one may need help choosing appropriate clothing, dressing, and undressing. The questions below can help you assess whether your loved one needs assistance with these tasks.

Checklist: *Assessing whether your loved one needs help with dressing*

- ☑ Does your loved one become confused when presented with too many choices?

- ☑ Does your loved one understand how to use buttons, zippers, and other fasteners appropriately?

- ☑ Does your loved one have the muscle control needed to put on their own clothes?

- ☑ Does your loved one recognize different parts of the body?

- ☑ Does your loved one know which order to put clothes on? For example, many individuals with Alzheimer's disease put their underwear on over their pants.

- ☑ Is your loved one able to choose clothes that match?

- ☑ Does your loved one choose clothing that is inappropriate for the weather?

- ☑ Does your loved one understand why they need to change clothes?

- ☑ Does your loved one put on dirty clothes that have been worn several times before?

☑ Does your loved one like the familiarity of old, dirty clothing?

☑ Is your loved one vision-impaired? This may contribute to not recognizing when clothing is dirty.

Once you have determined that your loved one needs help dressing, you will want to find ways to simplify the dressing process. This will require a two-pronged approach. First, you will need to find ways to narrow your loved one's clothing choices while still allowing them the freedom to be comfortable and feel good about the way they look. Second, you will need to provide physical assistance with getting dressed in a way that preserves your loved one's modesty and sense of independence. The following checklists provide some ideas for addressing these two areas.

Checklist: How to make it easier for your loved one to choose their clothing

☑ Move the clothing your loved one wears most often to an easily accessible location.

☑ Place matching outfits together in the closet or in drawers.

☑ Label each drawer with its contents and instructions for how to put on that item. Use pictures from a magazine if you think that will help.

☑ Remove busy patterns that may be distracting or annoying; stick with solid colors or simple patterns.

☑ Go through your loved one's closet and remove clothing they don't need because they no longer wear it, it doesn't fit, or it is the wrong season.

☑ Put extra clothing in a different room or closet, and move one or two choices into your loved one's closet each day.

☑ If you keep all your loved one's clothing in their closet, pull out two outfits and give them a choice of which one they want to wear.

☑ If your loved one is changing clothes multiple times per day, consider installing a lock on the closet.

☑ Purchase only comfortable cotton underwear or boxer shorts and sports bras or front-clasping bras, and remove all undergarments that may be restrictive, hard to put on, or cause chafing.

Checklist: *How to help your loved one dress*

☑ Allow your loved one to make clothing choices and participate in dressing as long as they are able. This helps them retain their own identity and sense of style.

☑ Choose clothing with few buttons and other fasteners. Jogging pants and sweatshirts or t-shirts will be the easiest for you and your loved one to handle. In the later stages of the disease when a caregiver dresses your loved one, choosing shirts with buttons in the front may be easier than slip-on shirts.

☑ Although clothing without fasteners may be easiest, if your loved one previously enjoyed wearing finer clothing, they may feel distress if they do not recognize the person in the mirror. Allow your loved one to wear clothing that eases their distress, even if it is harder to manage.

☑ Eliminate belts or other accessories that may be used incorrectly or dangerously.

☑ Choose or purchase pants with elastic waistbands.

☑ Use Velcro fasteners to replace other fasteners that may be difficult for your loved one to handle.

☑ Keep the same routine for dressing every day. For example, change clothes immediately after waking and again immediately before bed. For simplicity, you will likely want to couple dressing with taking a bath. Also, change tops and bottoms in the same order every day.

☑ Lay out your loved one's clothes in the order they should be put on.

☑ Make sure all needed items are at hand before your loved one begins dressing. They may abandon the idea of changing clothes if you have to leave the room.

☑ Stand behind your loved one to help them dress. This may lessen their awareness that you are helping, as well as their awareness of being naked in front of another individual.

☑ Use techniques to ensure your loved one's modesty, such as removing and replacing one piece of clothing at a time.

☑ Make sure that items are not inside out and that fasteners are undone before offering clothing to your loved one to put on.

☑ Allow your loved one plenty of time to dress. They will need more time than you would normally need, and they will need more time and more help as the disease progresses.

☑ Encourage your loved one to perform as many steps on their own as they can. Only intervene when they begin to get frustrated or it is obvious they will be unable to complete the task on their own.

☑ If your loved one makes a mistake when dressing, use humor to ease the situation without laughing at your loved one.

☑ As long as your loved one will have their pants removed anyway, ask if they need to use the toilet.

Credit: Ocskay Bence

☑ Allow your loved one to wear several layers of clothing if they wish, as long as they don't get overheated.

☑ Make sure your loved one is dressed appropriately for the temperature, especially if they are going outside.

☑ Choose clothing that is appropriate for coming activities. What your loved one is wearing may help them remember what they are doing. For example, dressing for shopping or church will require a different outfit than relaxing at home.

☑ Purchase shoes with Velcro rather than laces. This enables your loved one to put on their own shoes after they have forgotten how to tie shoelaces. It also prevents them from removing their laces and having their shoes fall off. This is a tripping hazard.

☑ Let your loved one sit while dressing to provide stability and prevent falls.

☑ If your loved one gets distracted by noise, turn off noise sources such as the TV or radio before changing clothes.

☑ If your loved one refuses your help, leave them alone for a little while and come back later to help them.

Your loved one may reach a point where they forget how to get dressed or undressed on their own. If this occurs, you will need to change your approach to the dressing process. A few ideas for doing so are presented in the following checklist.

Checklist: *How to deal with a loved one who has forgotten how to dress*

☑ Hand one piece of clothing to your loved one at a time and give instructions for how to put it on.

☑ Use gestures to demonstrate how to put on or take off each piece of clothing.

☑ If your loved one wears inappropriate items that may cause harm, consider putting away the items so your loved one does not have access to them.

☑ If your loved one chooses items of clothing that don't match or they wear clothing inappropriately (such as wearing a hat to bed), allow them to do so unless you feel it will cause them harm.

☑ If your loved one is unable to tell you if they are too hot or too cold, watch them for signs of discomfort and adjust clothing as needed. Layers may help regulate body temperature more easily.

☑ Remove soiled clothing from the room while your loved one is sleeping or bathing so they don't have the option of wearing the same clothes the next time they dress.

Eventually, your loved one may resist changing clothes, or simply refuse to do so. If this occurs, consider personal and environmental factors that may be contributing to the situation. Also, be flexible, particularly if the issue at hand will not negatively impact your loved one's personal hygiene. The checklist below offers some additional suggestions and ideas.

Checklist: *What do I do if my loved one refuses to change clothing?*

☑ Make sure the room is well-lit and warm. If the room is too cold, your loved one is more likely to resist removing clothing.

☑ Avoid telling your loved one that their clothes are dirty. Instead, suggest in a cheerful tone that it would be fun to wear something different today.

☑ Unless your loved one has already worn the same clothing multiple times and it is visibly dirty (or smells dirty), allow them to wear the same clothing for a few days if they want to. However, undergarments should be changed daily to prevent infection.

☑ If your loved one refuses to change clothing because they want to wear the same outfit all the time, buy multiple sets of your loved one's favorite outfit so they can wear one while you wash the other.

Credit: YsbrandCosjin

☑ If your loved one wears clothing to bed to prevent you from taking away their favorite outfit while they sleep, tell them when they get up that it is time to change out of their pajamas.

☑ Encourage your loved one to change because someone is coming to visit.

☑ Provide distractions while changing clothes, such as food or drink, TV, music, or photos.

Personal Hygiene and Grooming

Another ADL that is related to bathing and dressing is personal hygiene and grooming. As their disease progresses, your loved one may forget to perform grooming activities because they forget how to use the tools or forget that these activities should be performed regularly. They also may not understand why the activity needs to be done.

Some standard grooming activities are listed below, along with ways to assess whether your loved one needs help with grooming. When reviewing these, remember that each individual has a different list of grooming techniques that are important to them. For example, some people find it important to have their hair styled and nails painted, while others are fine with no nail polish and a simple hairstyle. Identify the activities your loved one has considered important in the past, and be prepared to balance those with their current capabilities.

Checklist: *Hygiene and grooming activities*

☑ Brushing and styling hair

☑ Brushing teeth

☑ Applying deodorant

☑ Shaving

☑ Applying aftershave or perfume

- ☑ Applying lotion to dry skin

- ☑ Cleaning and clipping fingernails and toenails

- ☑ Painting fingernails and toenails

- ☑ Applying makeup

- ☑ Cleaning dentures

- ☑ Cleaning eyeglasses

- ☑ Plucking unwanted hairs

- ☑ Cleaning ears

- ☑ Putting on jewelry

- ☑ Cutting hair

Checklist: *Assessing whether your loved one needs help with personal hygiene and grooming*

- ☑ Does your loved one frequently forget to brush their teeth (or clean their dentures) or comb their hair?

- ☑ Does your loved one recognize a toothbrush or comb and know what to do with it?

- ☑ Does your loved one remember how to shave?

- ☑ Can your loved one safely use a razor on their own?

- ☑ Does your loved one frequently forget to apply deodorant after a bath or when changing clothing?

- ☑ Does your loved one remember the purpose of a nail clipper?

- ☑ Does your loved one have dexterity problems that prevent them from grooming?

☑   Does your loved one forget the complicated steps involved with grooming?

☑   Does your loved one forget what they are doing before they complete the task?

☑   Does your loved one have bad breath?

☑   Are your loved one's fingernails or toenails abnormally long or dirty?

☑   Has your loved one grown a beard when he is normally clean-shaven?

If you determine that your loved one needs help with grooming activities, you must develop a grooming routine. Your routine should include the same activities in the same order each day. The routine should become part of the larger daily routine and should occur at the same time each day, such as immediately after getting up or immediately before going to bed. Non-daily activities, like cutting hair and trimming fingernails and toenails, must also be considered. The checklists below offer suggestions for helping your loved one with their grooming routine.

Checklist: *How to help your loved one perform grooming activities*

General:

☑   Perform grooming activities alongside your loved one, and have them mimic your actions.

☑   Use both verbal and nonverbal cues to remind your loved one how to perform grooming activities.

☑   If your loved one doesn't recognize a grooming tool, demonstrate how to use it.

☑   If your loved one refuses to perform a grooming activity, determine how necessary it is. Non-essential grooming activities (e.g., painting fingernails, applying makeup) can easily be skipped. However, essential grooming activities (e.g., brushing teeth) should be performed at least daily.

☑ If your loved one is more compliant with one caregiver than another, have the favored caregiver perform tasks that your loved one is most resistant to.

☑ If your loved one still refuses to perform a grooming activity, let it go. Try again later, because what is unacceptable now may be acceptable later.

☑ Acknowledge your loved one's efforts to look nice, because this will encourage them to repeat the action.

Teeth:

☑ Provide a thick-handled toothbrush that is easy to grasp.

☑ Try different types of toothbrushes to find one that is easiest for your loved one to tolerate. Do not use electric toothbrushes, as the vibration and noise may scare your loved one.

☑ Use the same brand of toothpaste that your loved one has always used. Add the toothpaste to the toothbrush for them.

☑ If your loved one refuses to brush their teeth, try using fluoride swabs rather than a toothbrush.

☑ If you are brushing your loved one's teeth, hold the toothbrush at a 45 degree angle to brush the gums along with the teeth.

☑ If your loved one clenches their teeth and won't open for brushing, brush as much as you can see.

☑ If it is possible to floss your loved one's teeth, do it regularly. However, do not risk being bitten if your loved one refuses to floss.

☑ If your loved one wears dentures, monitor their gums for sores that may indicate ill-fitting dentures. Use a soft toothbrush or moist cloth to clean their gums.

☑ Clean dentures twice daily following a dentist's instructions. Ask the dentist to teach you how to insert and remove dentures properly.

☑ If your loved one is able, provide them with apples or similar fresh fruit to aid in oral hygiene.

☑ If your loved one experiences dry mouth, try sugar-free candy or gum to increase saliva flow.

☑ Schedule a checkup with a dentist once or twice a year to check for cavities and other problems. Tell the dentist that your loved one has dementia so they should allow adequate time for the appointment. If necessary, find a dentist with experience caring for individuals with Alzheimer's disease.

☑ If your loved one becomes agitated or frightened when visiting the dentist, try to monitor their oral health at home and only take them to the dentist if they are in visible pain or have an obvious cavity.

Hair:

☑ Use the same hair styling products and hair style that your loved one is used to. Going with a different look may cause your loved one distress because they don't recognize their image in the mirror.

☑ Don't try to maintain an elaborate hairstyle unless it seems important to your loved one.

☑ Use as few hair products (gel, hairspray, mousse, etc.) as possible.

☑ If you are taking your loved one to a barber or hair stylist, let them know that your loved one has dementia and that they should book a longer appointment.

☑ While at the barber or hair salon, have the stylist shampoo your loved one's hair first, as this will likely be relaxing and will help the rest of the appointment go better.

☑ If needed, ask a hairstylist to come to your loved one's home to provide a haircut, wash, or style.

Shaving:

☑ When shaving, lay out all the needed tools and provide simple, step-by-step instructions.

☑ If shaving becomes difficult, allow your loved one to grow a beard.

Skin and nails:

☑ Use a gentle cleansing cloth or baby wipe to clean your loved one's face. This may be easier than using soap that must be rinsed off.

☑ Apply lotion to your loved one's skin after a bath to prevent dry and cracking skin.

☑ Use a favorite scented lotion, and perform a "massage" to rub it in.

☑ If your loved one enjoys having lotion applied, try doing this when your loved one is most restless.

☑ Check your loved one's feet regularly for signs of circulatory problems, such as a blue tinge to the feet and toes.

☑ Check your loved one's feet regularly for sores or other issues that might cause pain. This is especially important if your loved one has diabetes.

☑ If you see a wound on your loved one's skin, talk to a physician to learn ways to promote healing and prevent infection.

☑   Take your loved one to a podiatrist or a nail salon to clip their nails if you find this task difficult.

The nature of some grooming tools makes them potentially dangerous to your loved one. Other seemingly harmless items may also present hazards through misuse. As a result, you must consider your loved one's safety when developing a grooming routine. The checklist below provides a few ideas that may be helpful.

Checklist: *Grooming safety*

☑   Minimize the number of hygiene products in the bathroom. Some products may be misused, such as using shaving cream instead of toothpaste.

☑   Avoid mouthwash, which is swallowed too easily.

☑   Keep electric tools away from sources of running water to prevent electrocution. Some tools, such as an electric razor, hairdryer, or curling iron may be used in a bedroom with a mirror rather than in the bathroom.

☑   If your loved one will tolerate the noise and vibration, use an electric razor rather than a straight-edge razor to avoid nicks and cuts.

☑   Use a cardboard nail file rather than clippers to keep your loved one's nails tidy.

☑   For a woman who normally wears make-up, avoid using eye make-up that may get in their eyes and cause pain.

Toileting

Individuals with Alzheimer's disease commonly experience loss of bladder or bowel control, which results in difficulties with ADL related to toileting. Several factors contribute to this loss of control: individuals may forget their need to use the bathroom, they may forget the steps to toileting, or they may lose the physical ability to get to the bathroom on time. Medical problems, medications, and environmental factors may also contribute to toileting issues.

Dealing with incontinence and other toileting issues may be uncomfortable or embarrassing for you, but remember that your loved one is likely equally embarrassed. As a caregiver, your reactions can help lessen these feelings for both you and your loved one. In addition, your actions are essential to maintaining your loved one's health.

The questions below will help you assess whether your loved one needs assistance with toileting, and the subsequent checklist will help you implement steps to reduce toileting accidents and keep your loved one clean and free from infection.

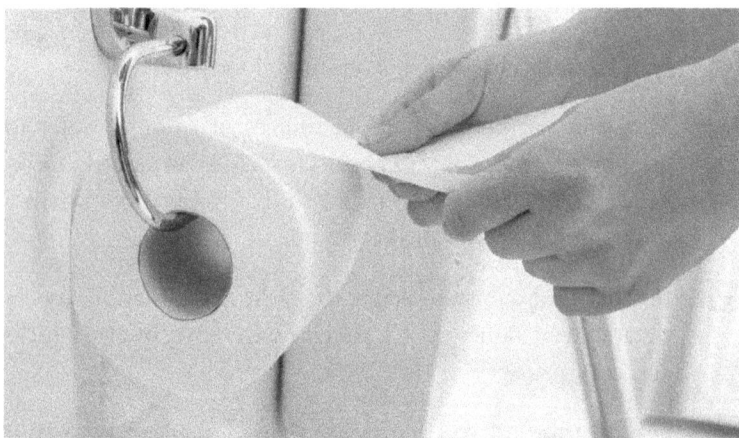

Credit: Andrey_Popov

Checklist: *Assessing whether your loved one needs help with toileting*

☑ Does your loved one remember where the bathroom is?

☑ Is your loved one able to react quickly to the urge to urinate?

☑ Does your loved one frequently fail to make it to the bathroom on time?

☑ Does your loved one have mobility problems that may prevent them from reaching the toilet in time?

☑ Is your loved one able to communicate their need to use the toilet?

☑ Does your loved one understand the purpose of the toilet?

☑ Does your loved one use the toilet only for going to the bathroom and not as a disposal for other items?

☑ Has your loved one forgotten the steps to using the toilet?

☑ Does your loved one remember to pull their pants down before using the toilet and pull them back up when they are done?

☑ Does your loved one remember to wipe thoroughly after using the toilet?

☑ Does your loved one remember to flush and wash their hands after using the toilet?

☑ Does your loved one understand the purpose of adult diapers or incontinence pads?

☑ Does your loved one urinate or defecate in inappropriate places, such as a closet or wastebasket?

☑ Does your loved one believe they are in the past and need to use an outhouse or other type of toilet?

☑ Does your loved one attempt to hide soiled clothing and then forget about it?

Checklist: *Tips for helping your loved one use the toilet*

☑ Watch your loved one for non-verbal cues (e.g., grimacing, holding themselves) that they need to use the bathroom.

☑ Learn your loved one's trigger words for needing to use the bathroom. They may say something like "I want to turn on the light" instead of telling you they need to use the toilet.

☑ Simplify clothing so it is easy to get on and off for toileting.

☑ Purchase a bell or buzzer that your loved one can ring if they have trouble getting to the bathroom.

☑ Treat your loved one like an adult rather than a child when helping them use the toilet.

☑ Be matter-of-fact when helping your loved one use the toilet to reduce discomfort about exposing their private areas.

☑ Allow as much privacy as your loved one's physical and mental abilities permit.

☑ Give your loved one plenty of time to completely empty their bladder and bowels.

☑ When your loved one is sitting on the toilet, run water to stimulate urination.

☑ If your loved one is hyperactive, allow them to get up and down from the toilet a few times before encouraging them to urinate or defecate.

☑ Give your loved one something to occupy their hands while urinating or defecating. This will provide a distraction to help them relax and go to the bathroom.

☑ Remind your loved one to wipe, flush, and wash their hands after they use the toilet.

☑ Use moist toilet tissues rather than dry. This helps your loved one stay cleaner and can allow them to go longer between baths if you have a hard time getting your loved one to bathe. Be aware that some individuals may develop a rash to some brands of moist wipes.

☑ If you notice any skin problems (e.g., rash, sores), treat them immediately.

☑ Keep the bathroom door open when not in use so the toilet is visible to your loved one.

☑ Use glow-in-the-dark tape to draw a direct line to the bathroom at night.

☑ If your loved one is going out, prepare by making sure you know where available toilets are, and have your loved one wear an incontinence pad.

As with other ADL, you will need to make safety modifications related to toileting. The bathroom presents special safety challenges because of the potential for surfaces to become wet and slippery and because of the presence of fixtures that are easily bumped into or tripped over. The list below presents some ideas for creating a safer bathroom environment for your loved one.

Checklist: *Toileting safety*

☑ Clear the path from your loved one's favorite chair and bed to the bathroom.

☑ Install lights in the bedroom, bathroom, and hallways so your loved one can safely make it to the bathroom at night.

☑ Remove or secure rugs that may cause your loved one to slip.

☑ If the bathroom is uncarpeted, place adhesive strips or decals on the floor near the toilet and sink.

☑ Use a raised toilet seat and hand rails to provide balance and help with standing and sitting.

☑ If your loved one is a man, consider encouraging him to sit rather than stand when he urinates, especially if he has trouble with balance or aim.

Confusion related to toileting can lead to both safety issues and problems with reaching the bathroom in time. Simple home modifications that help reduce confusion can decrease the likelihood of injury and accidents. The following checklist offers some suggestions for dealing with confusion in the bathroom.

Checklist: *Dealing with confusion*

☑ Paint the bathroom door so it is easier to find.

☑ Label the bathroom door so your loved one can easily find the bathroom if they are confused. Use a picture if that helps.

☑ Paint the wall behind the toilet a dark color so the toilet is easier to see. Use a contrasting color for the toilet seat compared to the base.

☑ Post instructions by the toilet in case your loved one forgets the steps for going to the bathroom.

☑ Remove plants, wastebaskets, and other items that may be mistaken for a toilet.

☑ Check the placement of mirrors in relation to the toilet. Your loved one may not urinate if they believe the toilet is occupied by someone else.

Eventually, even with modifications and assistance with toileting, your loved one may experience incontinence. This can be upsetting to both you and your loved one, and one of the biggest barriers to dealing with incontinence is the caregiver's attitude.

You must take charge of yourself and the situation—both mentally and emotionally—and remain positive and reassuring for your loved one's sake. Doing so will make things go much more smoothly and will help you overcome your feelings of embarrassment. The following list offers a few suggestions for handling incontinence.

Checklist: *Dealing with incontinence*

☑ Use scheduled toileting to prevent incontinence. Scheduled toileting involves taking your loved one to the toilet at regular intervals, usually about every two hours. Scheduled toileting before and after meals, before bedtime, and after getting up in the morning is also recommended.

☑ Monitor when accidents occur, and get your loved one to the bathroom before they normally have an accident.

☑ React calmly when accidents occur, and treat your loved one with dignity. Remember, the accident is a result of the disease, and your loved one did not intentionally make a mess.

☑ Reassure your loved one when they have an accident. Refer to it as a "spill" rather than telling them they wet themselves.

☑ Be ready for accidents and set up the house for quick cleaning.

☑ Change clothing and diapers as soon as possible after incontinence occurs.

☑ Make sure your loved one washes and dries thoroughly before putting on new clothes.

☑ Wash soiled clothing, sheets, and other items immediately.

☑ Don't scold your loved one after an accident. They likely already feel guilty or embarrassed.

☑ Treat the use of adult diapers or incontinence pads as just another step in the dressing process. Don't associate these products with shame or embarrassment.

☑ Encourage your loved one to wear adult diapers or incontinence pads if they leave the house for an extended period of time.

☑ Keep a supply of adult diapers or underwear pads close to the toilet for your loved one to use. Your loved one may need assistance getting diapers on and off.

☑ Purchase inexpensive, washable chair cushion covers to put on your loved one's favorite chair or recliner. Cover the cushions with trash bags, and slip a cushion cover over the bags for waterproofing.

☑ Use a waterproof bed pad to protect your loved one's mattress from nighttime accidents.

☑ Consider putting a commode in the bedroom for nighttime use.

☑ Replace drinks that may irritate the bladder (e.g., coffee, tea, cola, alcohol) with non-irritating drinks (e.g., water, fruit drinks, herbal teas).

☑ Limit fluids for two hours before bed, but offer a drink if your loved one is genuinely thirsty.

☑ Do not withhold fluids from your loved one if they are incontinent. This may lead to dehydration and urinary tract infections.

☑ If incontinence is a recent development, consult a physician about possible causes. Urinary tract infections, medications, constipation, prostate enlargement, and other medical issues may contribute to incontinence.

☑ Be aware that individuals with Alzheimer's disease often suffer from overactive bladder, which causes a sudden and intense urge to urinate. They may also suffer from frequency, which is urinating often, and from stress incontinence, which is leaking urine after sneezing or coughing.

☑ If your loved one doesn't even make an attempt to find a toilet when they need to urinate or defecate, they may be suffering from depression. Consult a physician or mental health worker.

☑ If your loved one is incontinent, apply an ointment such as Vaseline around their rectum, vagina, or penis after their bath.

☑ Remember that urine and feces will not harm you if handled properly.

Whether your loved one requires assistance with toileting or is incontinent, make yourself aware of when and how often they must urinate or defecate. This can help you know when a bathroom trip may be needed, and it can also help you detect irregularities with your loved one's normal elimination pattern.

Constipation and urinary tract infection (UTI) are two elimination issues that commonly affect individuals with Alzheimer's disease. Both of these conditions can worsen existing toileting issues; coincidentally, both of them can also be worsened by toileting issues. The nature of these relationships makes it very important for caregivers to be observant and act quickly if they notice a problem. The checklists below provide information about identifying and handling constipation and UTI.

Checklist: Dealing with constipation

☑ Watch your loved one for signs of constipation (i.e., track bowel movements and make sure they follow your loved one's normal pattern). If you note any issues, alert a physician.

☑ Be aware that strong negative reactions to or fear of using the bathroom may indicate your loved one is constipated, especially if the fear develops suddenly.

☑ Understand that changes in medication can sometimes trigger or worsen constipation. Be on the lookout for constipation indicators any time your loved one's prescriptions change.

☑ Make note if your loved one mentions pain when they defecate. Pain may indicate constipation or fecal impaction.

☑ If your loved one rarely defecates in the toilet but often has soiled underwear, they may be constipated. Small leakage of liquid stool can indicate constipation.

☑ Consult a physician if you suspect your loved one is constipated. The physician may be able to suggest a laxative or other product to relieve the constipation.

☑ Make sure your loved one eats enough fresh fruits and vegetables to provide adequate fiber for regular bowel movements. Don't go overboard, though; too much fiber can cause diarrhea.

☑ Note that proper hydration can reduce the chance of developing constipation. Encourage your loved one to consume a sufficient amount of liquid each day.

☑ If possible, help your loved one engage in regular exercise, as this can help promote bowel movements and prevent constipation.

☑ Set a time each day to have your loved one defecate. Have them sit on the toilet until they defecate. This time should reflect your loved one's normal elimination pattern if you know it. For example, many people defecate right after eating breakfast.

☑ Remember that some individuals only defecate two to three times a week. Your loved one's bowel movement patterns should be the same before and after they develop Alzheimer's disease.

Checklist: *Dealing with urinary tract infections*

UTI Basics

☑ A urinary tract infection occurs when bacteria enter the urinary tract, including the urethra (tube from bladder to outside the body), ureter (tube from kidneys to bladder), bladder, or kidneys.

☑ Women are more susceptible to UTIs than men because their urethra is shorter.

☑ Complications are uncommon, but if the infection spreads to the blood it can be fatal.

☑ UTIs can speed the decline of someone with dementia or Alzheimer's disease.

☑ Problems emptying the bladder (e.g., due to an enlarged prostate) may contribute to UTIs.

☑ Individuals with weak immune systems (e.g., people with diabetes or people who are being treated for cancer) are more susceptible to UTIs.

Typical Signs of a UTI

☑ Cloudy urine

☑ Blood in the urine

☑ Pain during urination

☑ Foul-smelling urine

☑ Lower abdominal pain

☑ Fever

☑ Nausea or vomiting

☑ Shaking or chills

Common Signs of a UTI in Individuals with Alzheimer's Disease

☑ Rapid increase in confusion

☑ Agitation

☑ Withdrawal

☑ Decreased appetite

☑ Increased time spent sleeping

☑ Decreased balance control

☑ Increased incidence of falls

☑ Sudden decrease in the ability to complete tasks

☑   Violent or odd behavior

Preventing UTIs

☑   Wipe from front to back rather than back to front.

☑   Change soiled diapers as frequently as needed. Do not let your loved one remain in wet diapers or clothing. Being exposed to wet material for a long time can cause skin breakdown and infection.

☑   Avoid the use of catheters if your loved one continues to have problems with incontinence, because UTIs are much more common in individuals with catheters.

☑   Watch your loved one for signs of dehydration (i.e., check the color of their urine; dark yellow urine indicates dehydration). Dehydration may lead to urinary tract infections.

☑   Make sure your loved one's genitals are cleansed daily and that their underwear are changed daily.

☑   Make sure your loved one drinks between six and eight glasses of fluids each day. To encourage this behavior, keep your loved one's favorite drinks on hand. Individuals with Alzheimer's disease often forget that they need to drink, so you may need to remind them.

☑   Prompt your loved one to empty their bladder several times a day. Holding urine in the bladder can promote UTIs.

☑   Some evidence indicates that drinking cranberry juice can help prevent UTIs.

Treating UTIs

☑   See a physician as soon as possible if you suspect your loved one has a UTI.

☑ Your loved one's physician will likely request a urine specimen. Upon confirmation of the infection with the specimen, the physician will likely prescribe an antibiotic for your loved one.

☑ If your loved one is given an antibiotic to treat their UTI, make sure they take the full course of medication prescribed by the physician. Not taking all of the antibiotics could lead to recurring infections and bacterial resistance to antibiotics.

☑ If the UTI is caused by a physical problem such as an enlarged prostate, the physician may recommend surgery to take care of the problem.

☑ If your loved one has recurring UTIs, they may be referred to a urologist.

Eating

Eating is a vitally important ADL and one with many complicating factors for individuals with Alzheimer's disease. Changes in cognitive function often mean that individuals forget to eat, forget to go grocery shopping, or forget how to cook. Some individuals also suffer from a loss of appetite, a loss of motivation to eat, or difficulty controlling swallowing muscles. As a result, weight loss is common in individuals with Alzheimer's disease. In my father's case, he never really cooked. He used the microwave frequently, but he was unable to complete even this simple task after he developed Alzheimer's disease. However, he loved to eat out, so we ate out often. Eventually, he did not know how to order or how sauces were used. For example, I would frequently stop him from trying to eat salsa as a soup or trying to drink soup straight from the bowl.

Changes that are typical of the aging process also affect individuals with Alzheimer's disease. For example, older people often experience changes in their sense of taste or smell that affect their eating habits. Activity levels also tend to decline in older people, causing a decline in food intake.

These issues combine to make meals a challenge for people with Alzheimer's disease. They also make a caregiver's help with eating vitally important. The questions below will help you assess your loved one's need for assistance with eating.

Checklist: *Assessing whether your loved one needs help with eating*

☑ Is your loved one able to communicate their need for food or drink, or express their desire for a specific type of food?

☑ Does your loved one seem overwhelmed by the food choices available to them?

☑ Is the food available something that your loved one likes to eat?

☑ Does your loved one get too distracted to eat?

☑ Does your loved one seem disinterested in eating?

☑ Is your loved one drinking so much that they are no longer hungry?

☑ Has your loved one lost their sense of taste or smell?

☑ Do your loved one's dentures fit properly, or do they come loose while eating?

☑ Does your loved one remember how to transfer food to their plate?

☑ Can your loved one put food on their plate without making a mess?

☑ Does your loved one have coordination problems when handling silverware?

☑ Is your loved one able to cut large portions (such as a piece of meat) into bite-size pieces?

☑ Has your loved one forgotten how to feed themselves?

☑ Does your loved one have a problem with swallowing or choking?

☑ Does your loved one have delusions about the food being poisoned?

☑ If your loved one is in a group setting, do they allow others to eat their food?

After identifying your loved one's areas of need, you must determine how best to encourage them to eat. This may require mealtime modifications that affect you and other family members as well as your loved one. The flexibility of everyone at your table will help you ensure proper nutrition for your loved one. The following checklist includes some suggestions for getting started with this process.

Checklist: *Techniques to help your loved one eat*

☑ Establish a mealtime routine. Eat at the same times and in the same place every day.

☑ Minimize distractions by serving meals in a quiet location. Turn off the TV and radio, and make sure lighting is adequate.

☑ Have your loved one eat with others. This makes meals a social event your loved one looks forward to and provides your loved one with opportunities to watch others for clues about how to eat.

☑ Make sure your loved one is equipped with items that will help them eat, such as properly fitting dentures and eyeglasses with a correct prescription.

☑ Choose dishes and utensils that enable your loved one to eat independently. Spoons and forks with larger handles, cups with lids and straws, and bowls may make eating easier for your loved one.

Credit: Pressmaster

☑ Use easily distinguishable place settings. Placemats and dishes in contrasting colors are easier to tell apart, and white or solid-color dishes make food easier to identify.

☑ Serve precut food or finger food if your loved one has difficulty using utensils.

☑ Make sure food is served at an appropriate temperature. Food that is too hot may burn the tongue, and food that is too cold may be unappetizing.

☑ If your loved one is unable to feed themselves, prompt them to eat by raising food to their mouth and instructing them to open their mouth.

☑ Give your loved one foods that they like to eat, but make sure to offer a variety of favorite foods from day to day. Serving the same food over and over because it is well-tolerated may negatively impact nutrition.

☑ If your loved one seems confused or overwhelmed by too many choices, serve one type of food at a time.

☑ Allow plenty of time for meals. Do not rush your loved one or otherwise hurry through the meal.

☑ Check that your loved one's mouth is empty before eating, especially if your loved one tends to hoard things.

☑ If your loved one believes the food is poisoned, reassure them that you would not offer them poisoned food, and try a bite to demonstrate that the food is not poisoned.

☑ Provide snacks throughout the day if your loved one appears hungry.

☑ If your loved one loses significant weight, consult a physician. The physician may suggest nutritional supplements or refer you to a nutritionist.

If your loved one has a poor appetite, mealtime modifications alone may not be enough to increase nutritional intake. Depending upon the degree of your loved one's disinterest in food, you may need to consult with a physician to determine causes and solutions. The following checklist offers some ideas for improving appetite.

Checklist: How to increase your loved one's appetite

☑ Have your loved one assessed for problems that may be decreasing their appetite, such as stomach ulcers, heartburn, or depression. Treating the underlying cause of decreased appetite will help increase appetite.

☑ Ask your loved one's physician or pharmacist if any of your loved one's medications can cause a loss of appetite. Altering the dose of a medication or switching to a different medication may help increase your loved one's appetite.

☑ Check for sores or bleeding in your loved one's mouth. Ill-fitting dentures or painful teeth or gums can make eating uncomfortable. Consult with your loved one's dentist if you notice anything unusual, and maintain regular oral care.

☑ Serve meals or snacks when your loved one is rested and alert. Tiredness can impact concentration and coordination and make it difficult for your loved one to eat.

☑ Encourage your loved one to be more active if they are able. Increased physical activity can increase appetite. Taking a walk or engaging in light exercise may be beneficial.

☑ Assess your loved one for signs of constipation. Constipation may make your loved one feel bloated and nauseous, which will make them averse to eating.

☑ Monitor your loved one's fluid intake. If they are drinking a lot before meal time, they may not be hungry for food.

☑ If your loved one tends to drink a lot at mealtime, allow them to eat several bites of food before offering a drink.

Swallowing difficulties may arise as Alzheimer's disease progresses and may also contribute to problems with eating. These difficulties—known as dysphagia—vary from person to person and may include holding food in the mouth without chewing and continuous chewing without swallowing. The following checklist offers suggestions for choking prevention.

Checklist: How to deal with swallowing difficulties and choking

☑ Have your loved one get a swallowing assessment from a speech therapist.

☑ Encourage your loved one to sit in an upright position while eating, and ensure that they are alert.

☑ Serve foods that are soft rather than those that are hard or difficult to chew. Foods like scrambled eggs, applesauce, and cooked carrots will be much easier for your loved one than steak, whole apples, and raw carrots.

☑ If soft foods alone are not enough, ask a physician or dietician if pureed food is appropriate. When pureeing food, select items with good flavor and pleasing color.

☑ Offer thick drinks like shakes or smoothies to increase caloric intake.

☑ Learn the Heimlich maneuver in order to help your loved one should choking occur.

Communication

At first glance, communication may seem less critical to physical wellbeing than the other ADL we've already discussed; in reality, though, it is extremely important to your loved one's health. Bathing, grooming, toileting, and eating are all impacted by your loved one's ability to communicate with you, as well as their ability to understand how you are communicating with them. Communication ability also impacts your loved one's emotional well-being.

Communicating with a loved one who has Alzheimer's disease is challenging. Your loved one is likely aware of—and distressed by—their change in abilities, particularly in the mild and moderate stages of the disease. You may feel distressed and frustrated, too; try to control these emotions as best you can. Remember, it's not just what you say, but how you say it. If your loved one senses negative emotions in your tone or body language, they may mirror these emotions back to you. At this point, communication breaks down even further.

Confusion, anxiety, and irritability are subtle early indicators of communication difficulties. As your loved one's ability to communicate declines, more definitive indicators will develop. The questions below will help you assess your loved one's communication difficulties.

Checklist: Assessing your loved one's communication difficulties

☑ Does your loved one easily lose their train of thought mid-sentence?

☑ Does your loved one misuse common or familiar words?

☑ Does your loved one struggle to use words in a logical order?

☑ Has your loved one started repeating stories, phrases, or questions multiple times throughout the day?

☑ Does your loved one make up new words to describe familiar objects?

☑ Does your loved one talk in shorter sentences or phrases than was typical in the past?

☑ Has your loved one started speaking less often than was typical in the past?

☑ If your loved one usually speaks in a second language, have they reverted to using their native language?

☑ Has your loved one started speaking nonsense?

☑ Does your loved one understand what you are saying without asking you to repeat yourself?

☑ Is your loved one able to follow simple verbal or written directions?

☑ Does your loved one respond appropriately to questions?

☑ Is your loved one able to follow a conversation and contribute to it?

You may want to refer back to these questions periodically to assess ongoing changes to your loved one's communication. Their capabilities will change as the disease progresses, and their ability to understand and speak will becoming increasingly impaired. As a result, you must be a careful observer of what does and does not work when communicating with your loved one. Remember, too, that techniques that worked in the past may no longer be effective. The following checklists offer suggestions for communicating with your loved one in the mild, moderate, and severe stages of Alzheimer's disease. No matter what stage your loved one is in, bear in mind that calm and pleasant communication that reassures your loved one is essential.

Checklist: *How to communicate with your loved one with mild Alzheimer's disease*

☑ When starting a conversation, approach your loved one from the front and say their name to get their attention.

☑ Speak slower than normal and enunciate your words.

☑ Use short sentences and common, plain words. Sentences should only include one main thought.

☑ If asking questions, ask only one at a time and allow sufficient time for your loved one to answer.

☑ Avoid open-ended questions. Use yes-or-no questions or questions with limited choices.

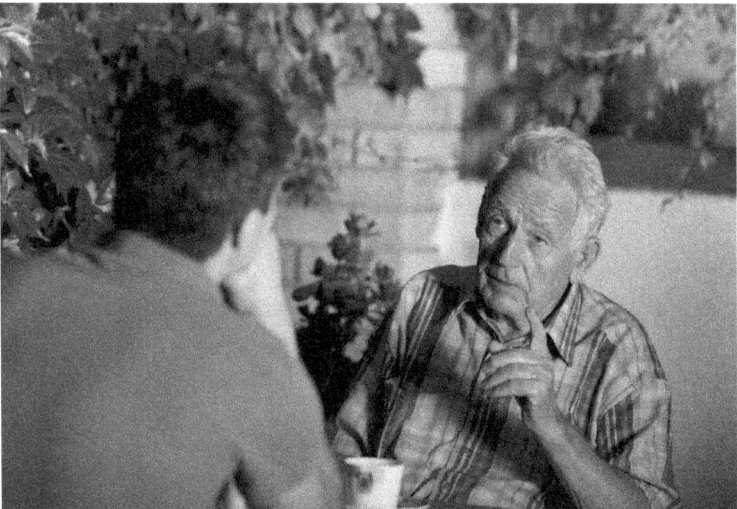

Credit: Budimir Jevtic

☑ Allow your loved one plenty of time to think about what you've said. Trying to fill the silence may cause confusion or agitation for your loved one.

☑ Be willing to repeat what you said multiple times until your loved one seems to understand. If you must repeat something, repeat it exactly the same way you said it the first time. Rephrasing your sentence will likely cause even more confusion. If this doesn't work after three attempts, try using simpler words and phrases.

☑ Be willing to listen to the same story or answer the same question multiple times. Do not point out that your loved one already said the same thing previously.

☑ Give instructions one step at a time.

☑ Use a pleasant tone when speaking. Avoid speaking loudly unless your loved one is hard of hearing.

☑ Use positive nonverbal communication (e.g., nodding, smiling, pointing) and avoid negative nonverbal communication (e.g., scowling, crossing your arms).

☑ Refer to people by name and relationship rather than by pronoun (e.g., your daughter, Jane).

☑ Use simple, consistent labels for objects (e.g., your brown rocking chair, your white tennis shoes).

☑ Stick to familiar or favorite topics for conversation.

☑ Be willing to carry the bulk of the conversation.

☑ Provide information rather than asking for information.

☑ Reduce background distractions, such as the TV or radio.

☑ Avoid frequently correcting your loved one. If you understand the thought being expressed, don't worry about whether the words used to express it are correct. If you don't understand, try repeating it back to help clarify the thought.

☑ Avoid statements that seem negative. For example, instead of saying, "Don't eat that," offer your loved one something else and say, "I think you'll like this better."

☑ Use humor when possible, but not at your loved one's expense.

☑ Use cards and letters to communicate in addition to personal visits or phone calls. This gives your loved one something to help them remember.

☑ Use a notebook to create a calendar of past events. For example, you may write that someone visited or that the trash was picked up that day.

☑ Try not to be discouraged or frustrated with communication difficulties. They are a part of the disease, and they are not your loved one's fault. Showing your frustration will discourage your loved one from trying to communicate and may make them withdraw from social situations.

Checklist: How to communicate with your loved one with moderate Alzheimer's disease

☑ Make sure your loved one can see and hear you. If your loved one wears glasses or uses a hearing aid, check that these items are in place. Try to talk in a quiet environment with minimal distractions.

☑ Rely on nonverbal communication when possible. Use visual cues to relay emotions and instructions.

☑ Gently touch your loved one's shoulder, back, or arm and make eye contact to maintain their attention and reassure them.

☑ Speak in answers, rather than questions. Instead of asking, "Are you hungry?" try saying, "I brought you some crackers."

☑ If your loved one isn't making sense, put the emphasis on "I." For example, you may say, "I'm sorry. I'm having a hard time understanding." They may be more clear the next time.

☑ Avoid questions that test your loved one's memory, especially their recent memory. Reminiscing can be healthy, but saying things like, "Do you remember?" can result in frustration and sadness for your loved one.

☑ Allow your loved one to "have their way" if they say something you do not agree with. Arguing with your loved one may cause them to become frustrated and will make you both feel bad.

☑ Listen and watch for emotions. Your loved one's tone and actions may more accurately convey their feelings than their words do.

☑ Remember that decreased verbal communication does not necessarily mean decreased awareness. Your loved one may feel distress about their lost abilities, and your continued efforts to engage them may ease these feelings.

Checklist: How to communicate with your loved one with severe Alzheimer's disease

☑ Comfort your loved one if they are having trouble communicating. Let them know it's ok and encourage them to continue expressing their thoughts in whatever way they are able. Be supportive and reassuring.

☑ Encourage nonverbal communication. Ask your loved one to point or gesture if you don't understand what they are saying or if they can no longer speak.

☑ Carry on a conversation, even if your loved one is unable to respond. This shows them that you care. Talk about subjects your loved one enjoys and mention family and friends by name.

☑ If you are unsure what to say, consider reading a passage from your loved one's favorite book, singing a song they enjoy, or looking at familiar photos and describing the scene.

☑ Speak to your loved one with respect and dignity. Never talk down to them or talk about them to others if they are in the room.

Mobility

Mobility is another ADL that is impacted by Alzheimer's disease. Individuals with the disease may develop problems with balance, gait, and movement. Similar to changes in communication, changes in mobility impact your loved one's ability to perform other ADL, such as dressing and toileting. Other medical conditions—such as stroke or arthritis—may further impact mobility and increase the likelihood of falls and injury.

In the early stages of Alzheimer's disease, simple home modifications like securing or removing rugs and minimizing clutter may be sufficient for helping your loved one move about safely. As time goes on, use of assistive devices such as a walker or cane may be necessary. Many of the assistive devices geared toward the aging population in general are also appropriate for individuals with Alzheimer's disease. If you are unsure whether a device is suited to your loved one, discuss it with their physician.

An early indicator of mobility difficulties is the development of a shuffling or unsteady walk. Decreased walking speed and increased clumsiness are other indicators. The questions below will help you assess whether your loved one is experiencing mobility difficulties.

Checklist: Assessing whether your loved one needs help with mobility

☑ Is your loved one having coordination problems that affect their ability to write or use familiar objects?

☑ Does your loved one frequently drop or knock over objects?

☑ Does your loved one tend to bump into furniture, walls, or people when walking?

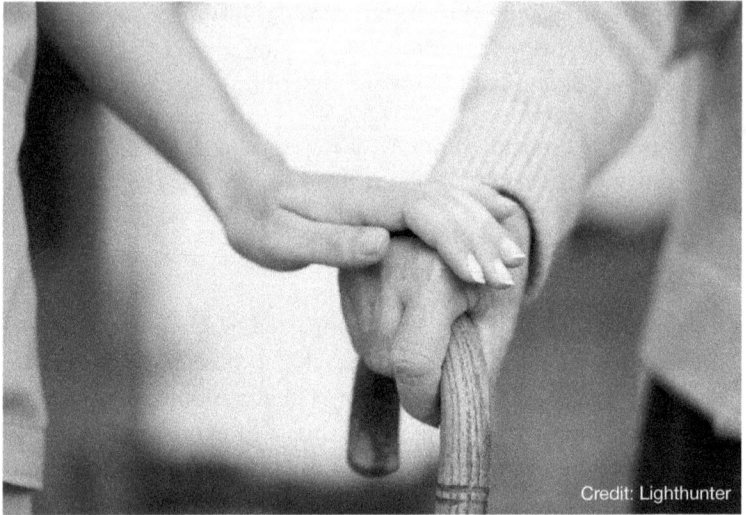

Credit: Lighthunter

☑ Would you describe your loved one's movements to others as being uncoordinated?

☑ Does your loved one often seem to trip over their own feet?

☑ Has your loved one fallen while walking or climbing stairs recently?

☑ Does your loved one have problems walking on uneven or sloping surfaces?

☑ Is your loved one able to walk only limited distances before stopping and resting?

☑ Does your loved one have difficulty getting out of chairs or beds?

☑ Does your loved one attempt to sit down on a chair that is not there?

☑ Is your loved one more comfortable or more steady when walking with another person rather than walking alone?

☑ Does your loved one tend to lean backward when walking?

☑ Does your loved one complain of muscle pain or stiffness?

As your loved one's illness progresses, their mobility status will change, as will their need for assistance. Walking will be one of the first areas in which assistance will be necessary. Home modifications and assistive devices may be useful, but it is a good idea to understand how best you can safely and effectively help your loved one move around their environment. The checklist below offers some strategies and techniques that may be useful.

Checklist: *Mobility strategies and techniques*

☑ Ask your loved one's physician if your loved one could benefit from physical or occupational therapy. Therapy can improve your loved one's strength, endurance, and range of motion and enable them to move independently longer.

☑ Install handrails in stairwells, bathrooms, and long hallways. Rails provide support and may encourage your loved one to continue moving in the direction of the rail. Rails must be securely anchored to walls.

☑ Ensure that your loved one is wearing sturdy shoes with a no-skid bottom. Shoes should fit snugly and be fastened.

☑ Provide a walking aid like a cane or walker. Make sure your loved one understands how to use the aid and that the aid has secure, no-skid feet.

☑ Offer assistance if your loved one is reluctant or unable to use the walking aid. Stand next to your loved one so you are both facing the same direction and walk in unison.

☑ If your loved one begins shuffling their feet while you are assisting them, encourage them to march as they walk. Humming a tune or tapping out a rhythm with your free hand may help.

☑ If you are assisting your loved one and their steps start to stutter or they pick up and set down a foot multiple times without taking a step, stop and restart by stepping. It may be helpful for you to take a long stride or "goose step" to provide a visual cue on the restart.

☑ If your loved one must climb up stairs, stand at their side facing the same direction. Ask them to hold the rail on the side opposite you. Have them place their whole foot on the step and then bring their other foot up to the same step, rather than alternating feet.

☑ If your loved one must climb down stairs, ask them to hold the same rail with both hands and come down sideways. Stand behind them and offer support and assistance as needed.

☑ In the early stages of mobility difficulties, encourage your loved one to walk longer distances to help them get into a walking rhythm. Pleasant conversation and a lot of personal attention will make the walk enjoyable and encourage your loved one to keep going.

☑ As mobility issues advance, your loved one may need to cover short distances at a time. Provide easily visible resting places along the way and allow your loved one to stop if they are tired.

☑ If your loved one refuses to walk or stops mid-walk and won't move, don't force them. Allow your loved one to rest, and try again in a little while. Never pull, push, or "tow" your loved one to prompt them to move. Doing so may cause them to fall or become agitated.

☑ Do not attempt to walk with your loved one if you notice them leaning backward. This could be dangerous.

☑ If your loved one begins to fall while you are walking with them, do your best to guide them slowly to the floor. Try getting behind them and sliding them down your body as they fall to help prevent injuries.

Your loved one may also require assistance standing up, sitting down, and lying down. In addition, some individuals with Alzheimer's disease become confined to a bed or chair. Utilizing proper transferring techniques is essential in these situations to prevent injury to you and your loved one. The checklist below offers examples of transferring techniques; before using any such technique, speak to your loved one's physician or therapist about the best techniques for your situation.

Checklist: *Techniques for transferring your loved one*

☑ When helping your loved one get up from a sitting position, ask them to place their hands on the armrests of the chair and their feet flat on the floor. Feet should be hip-width apart and below the knees. Have your loved one lean forward so their upper body is over their knees. Stand to the side of and behind your loved one, with feet spread in a lunge. Place one hand on their shoulder and the other across the lower back and hips. Rock forward together and bring your loved one to a standing position. Verbal cues like "ready, set, stand" may be helpful to the process.

☑ When helping your loved one sit from a standing position, ask them to put the back of their legs against the chair and lean forward while bending at the hips. Have them gently lower into the chair while reaching for the arms. Place a hand on your loved one's hip to guide and steady them. If your loved one is hesitant to sit without being able to see the chair, allow them to sit down sideways. Once they are seated, tap or place your hands on their hips to help your loved one turn so their back is against the chair back.

☑ When helping your loved one move from a chair to a wheelchair (or vice versa), make sure the wheels on the wheelchair are locked and the foot and arm rests are moved out of the way. Place the wheelchair close to the chair and at a right angle. Using the same technique for getting up from a sitting position, help your loved one stand. Allow them to find their balance before turning so the back of their legs is against the front of the wheelchair. Then, using the same technique for sitting from a standing position, have them sit down. If it is difficult for your loved one to gain their balance when transferring, allow them to use a walker for support.

☑ When helping your loved one move from lying down in a bed to sitting on the edge, ask them to bend their knees and roll onto their side. Have them put their legs over the edge of the bed and use their elbow to push their upper body upright while lowering their legs to the floor. Depending on their upper body strength, you may need to assist and steady your loved one as they come upright.

☑ When helping your loved one move from sitting on the edge of a bed to lying down, ask them to lean toward the head of the bed and support their weight on their elbow. Have them bring their bent legs up onto the bed. Allow them to turn onto their back and lower their legs. Depending on their upper body strength, you may need to assist and steady your loved one as they lower their weight onto their elbow.

☑ Be aware that your loved one is at risk for pressure sores if they are confined to a bed or chair. Pressure sores, sometimes called pressure ulcers or bedsores, are areas of damaged skin. They usually appear where the bones are closest to the skin when a person stays in one position for too long. Pressure sores can cause serious infections. Helping your loved one change positions regularly can reduce the likelihood of pressures sores. If you notice that your loved one has a pressure sore, speak to their physician about proper treatment and prevention strategies.

Instrumental ADL

In addition to ADL that relate directly to physical health and well-being, a second category of activities known as instrumental activities of daily living—or IADL—are important for maintaining an independent lifestyle. Typically, IADL involve more complex skills or combinations of skills than ADL.

In some ways, it can be easier for caregivers to find alternatives for IADL that can no longer be performed and easier for loved ones to accept assistance in these areas because these activities are less personal in nature than many ADL. However, because IADL are linked to independence, they present their own special set of challenges. IADL include activities from shopping and cooking to housekeeping and money management, to name a few.

Shopping

Shopping for food, clothing, and personal items is a normal part of daily life. Across the lifespan, people have differing attitudes about shopping—some love it, some hate it. This may hold true for your loved one after their diagnosis: If they enjoyed shopping before, they may continue to do so; if they did not, they still may not.

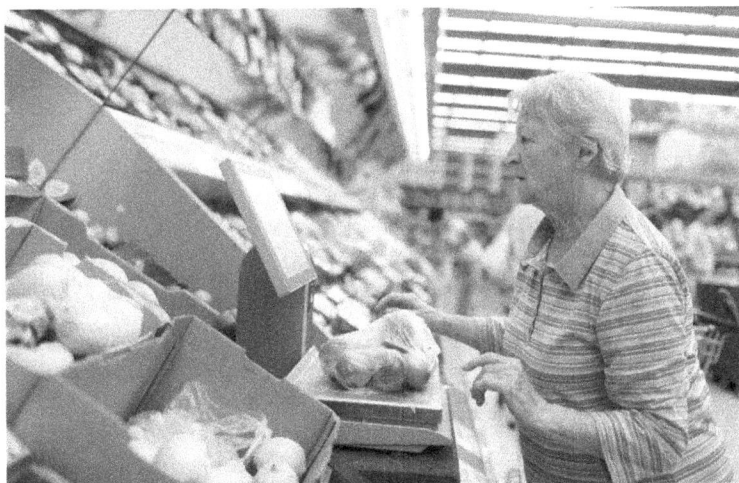

Credit: Canon Boy

Understanding your loved one's former shopping habits and preferences may help you identify whether they need assistance with their shopping chores. Changes in long-established habits may indicate a need, as may the absence of certain staple items your loved one always kept around the home. For example, if your loved one always had bananas in the fruit basket but has been without for several weeks, they may not be regularly visiting the grocery store. The questions below will help you assess whether your loved one needs some assistance with shopping chores.

Checklist: *Assessing whether your loved one needs help with shopping*

- ☑ Is your loved one frequently without basic grocery items, like milk and bread?

- ☑ Is your loved one frequently without basic personal care items, like soap and deodorant?

- ☑ Do your loved one's clothes look more worn or shabby than is typical?

- ☑ Does your loved one know how to make a shopping list?

- ☑ Does your loved one get lost on the way to the grocery store?

- ☑ Is your loved one able to transport their groceries and other purchases home?

- ☑ Does your loved one wander away or get lost in a store?

- ☑ Does your loved one remember that they need to pay for purchases?

- ☑ Does your loved one remember how to pay for purchases?

- ☑ Does your loved one open their wallet and ask the cashier to take what they need?

When the time comes to help your loved one with shopping, it's a good idea to have a shopping plan in place before you leave the house. Know what stores you will visit and what items you will shop for. The checklist below offers some additional ideas for preparing for your shopping trip. In addition to these tips, remember that asking your loved one where they want to shop and allowing them to select their own items as much as possible is important for preserving independence.

Checklist: *Shopping with your loved one*

☑ Shop in places that are familiar to your loved one. Over time, staff at the store may come to recognize your loved one and understand their needs.

☑ Know where the quiet areas in the store are or where there is seating available in case your loved one needs to stop and take a break while shopping.

☑ Shop on the same day of the week and at the same time of day. Try to schedule your shopping time when your loved one is rested and at their most alert and when stores are at their least busy. Allow sufficient time for shopping and do not rush through it.

☑ If your loved one seems stressed at the scheduled shopping time, consider cancelling the trip and trying again on a different day or at a different time.

☑ When possible, stick with small stores. Large stores with a lot of customers or many choices may overwhelm your loved one.

☑ Look for shopping areas that have multiple stores that will be of use to your loved one. If, for example, the grocery store, pharmacy, and bank are all located in the same shopping area, you can complete your errands more quickly and easily.

☑ Keep a running list of items to purchase, and when your loved one runs out or runs low on a particular item, add it to the list. Keep the list and a pen in a visible, easily accessible place so your loved one can add to it. Magnetic list pads for the refrigerator are available at many stores.

☑ If purchasing groceries, make a meal plan and create a grocery list based on the plan. The plan should consider your loved one's preferences and dietary needs. It is also a good idea to plan for simple meals that are easy to prepare if your loved one will be doing the cooking.

☑ If purchasing clothing, check your loved one's size before buying. Weight gain or loss may have occurred without you realizing it. If your loved one will need to try clothes on, consider taking a same-gender caregiver along. Some stores may not allow women in the men's fitting room and vice versa.

☑ Know the layout of the stores you will visit, and try to organize your shopping list by aisle. This will make it easier for your loved one to find items as you move through the store.

☑ Remember that labels change and stores sometimes rearrange items. If your loved one seems confused as a result of such changes, offer support and reassurance.

☑ Look for home delivery options if your loved one is no longer willing or able to go to the store. Many cities have shopping services that will deliver groceries and other items to the home.

Cooking

As with shopping, cooking is an IADL that people tend to love or hate. If your loved one enjoys cooking, they may want to continue doing it as long as they are able; if your loved one does not enjoy cooking, they may be happy to hand over the responsibilities to you or a service like Meals on Wheels soon after their diagnosis.

No matter their outlook on cooking, your loved one will need to carry out basic kitchen tasks on a daily basis. You must understand and compensate for potential kitchen safety issues. In order to do so effectively, you will need to assess your loved one's ability to handle kitchen tasks independently. The questions below will help you assess your loved one's capabilities and determine whether they need assistance in the kitchen.

Checklist: *Assessing whether your loved one needs help with cooking*

☑ Does your loved one make appropriate food choices?

☑ Does your loved one understand which foods must be cooked and which foods can be eaten raw?

☑ Can your loved one tell the difference between good food and spoiled food?

☑ Does your loved one use appropriate ingredients when cooking or baking?

☑ Is your loved one able to follow a recipe?

☑ Can your loved one use the stove, oven, and microwave safely?

☑ Can your loved one safely use kitchen appliances, such as a coffee maker or can opener?

☑ Can your loved one safely handle knives?

☑ Can your loved one safely use the garbage disposal?

☑ Does your loved one store food in inappropriate locations (e.g., they put milk in a cabinet rather than the refrigerator)?

☑ Have you noticed missing or broken dishes in the kitchen?

☑ Have you noticed dirty dishes piling up in the sink?

Credit: StockLite

If your loved one requires assistance in the kitchen, try to make it an enjoyable experience. Cooking together is a good opportunity to share time and conversation. It can also be a positive way for your loved one to reminisce about the past, particularly if cooking is something you've regularly done together. Allow your loved one to take care of tasks that are within their capabilities, and volunteer to perform more difficult or potentially hazardous tasks yourself, such as chopping vegetables or using the gas stove.

Safety modifications to the kitchen are essential, even if you plan to help your loved one with all meal preparation. The concentration of potential hazards is especially high in the kitchen, and accidents can happen quickly, even if you are standing right next to your loved one. The checklist below offers some modifications and tips for promoting safety in the kitchen.

Checklist: *Safe cooking modifications and techniques*

☑ Remove spices, medicines, and any cleaning supplies from countertops and drawers. Move them out of the kitchen or place them in locked cabinets. Lock or remove the "junk drawer" from the kitchen.

☑ Remove scissors and knives from countertops and drawers. Purchase precut vegetables and meats or cut these items yourself and place them in the refrigerator for your loved one's use.

☑ Remove plastic or decorative fruit and magnets that are shaped like food to prevent them from mistakenly being eaten.

☑ Remove throw rugs, foam pads, and other tripping hazards from the kitchen floor.

☑ Replace breakable glasses and plates with plastic or other unbreakable items. If your loved one primarily cooks with the microwave, replace non-microwaveable pans and bowls with ones that are microwave safe.

☑ Set up a "cooking station" for your loved one. The station should be located away from the stove and other appliances and close to the items your loved one uses most.

☑ Keep commonly used items within easy reach to prevent climbing and reaching.

☑ Stock the refrigerator and pantry with easy-to-make food, such as sandwich materials or meals that can be made in the microwave.

☑ Stage items your loved one uses regularly. For example, if your loved one makes coffee every morning, prefill coffee filters with the right amount of grounds and place them in a container next to the coffee maker.

☑ Post clear instructions for use of kitchen appliances, such as the stove, microwave, and coffee maker. This will help your loved one know how to use these appliances if they get confused or cannot remember what to do.

☑ Install safety knobs to prevent your loved one from turning on the stove when you are not there, or purchase an automatic stove control device. The device includes a motion detector and can be programmed to shut the stove off when your loved one leaves the kitchen.

☑ Purchase an electric kettle with an automatic shut-off feature so your loved one can make tea or instant coffee without having to turn on the stove.

☑ Disable the garbage disposal and disguise the power switch.

☑ Keep small electric appliances away from the sink or other water sources, and unplug them when not in use.

☑ Place a drain trap in the kitchen sink to catch items that may fall down the drain. This will prevent items from becoming lost or clogging the drain.

☑ Label or color-code hot (red) and cold (blue) water faucets. Set the water heater to 120°F to avoid scalding.

☑ If your loved one is no longer able to use appliances safely, unplug them or turn off the circuit breakers that supply the power. Remove smaller items like electric can openers from the kitchen.

☑ Install smoke detectors and replace the batteries at least once each year. Keep fire extinguishers charged and easily accessible.

☑ Keep a first aid kit readily available. Post emergency and poison control numbers near the phone.

Housekeeping

Closely related to cooking is a group of IADL referred to as housekeeping. These activities include tasks like washing dishes and clothing, vacuuming, dusting, and cleaning kitchens and bathrooms. Basically, housekeeping chores are those tasks that keep your loved one's environment clean, healthy, and safe.

Seeking help with household tasks may signal a loss of independence to your loved one, which may make them hesitant to ask for assistance. As a result, you must make yourself aware of the chores that are not getting done and be prepared to lend a hand without taking over. Explain that your help will get the chores done faster and make time for more enjoyable activities, or suggest that working together will make the chores fun. The questions below will help you determine areas of housekeeping in which your loved one may need some help. Keep in mind that these questions should be asked in light of your loved one's normal housekeeping pattern from before they were diagnosed with Alzheimer's disease. For example, if your loved one never made their bed before, do not take an unmade bed as a sign of needing housekeeping help.

Checklist: Assessing whether your loved one needs help with housekeeping

☑ Does your loved one understand how to use housekeeping tools and products?

☑ Does your loved one remember how to do laundry?

☑ Do dirty clothes pile up in or around the hamper?

☑ Are clean clothes left out on dressers or chairs rather than being put away?

☑ Does your loved one remember to change and wash their bedding?

☑ Does your loved one leave the bed unmade?

☑ Does your loved one remember how to do dishes?

☑ Do dirty dishes pile up in and around the sink?

☑ Are clean dishes left out on the counter rather than being put away?

☑ Is there expired food in your loved one's refrigerator or cabinets?

☑ Do you notice unpleasant smells in the bathroom or kitchen?

☑ Are the bathroom sink, tub, and toilet noticeably dirty?

☑ Do garbage or recyclables pile up in or around trash cans or recycling bins?

☑ Is it evident that your loved one's home has not been vacuumed or dusted for several weeks?

☑ Is your loved one's house dirty or cluttered from lack of cleaning?

Every Alzheimer's patient is unique in their housekeeping needs and struggles. For example, your loved one's floor may go without vacuuming because they lack the upper body strength or balance and stability needed to push the vacuum. With a little prompting, however, they may be able to use the duster to clean the tops of tables and dressers. Working as a team with you vacuuming and your loved one dusting, you may be able to get a room or two clean over the course of an afternoon. The checklist below provides some suggestions for helping your loved one perform housekeeping tasks.

Checklist: *Housekeeping tips and techniques*

☑ Create a cleaning calendar and post it in a visible location. The calendar should include daily tasks like making the bed and putting dirty clothes in the hamper. It should also include weekly tasks, like dusting or doing laundry. Create a routine around daily tasks and schedule weekly tasks for the same day and time each week.

☑ Post clear instructions for use of cleaning appliances, such as the washer, dryer, or vacuum. This will help your loved one know how to use these appliances if they get confused or cannot remember what to do.

☑ Identify tasks that you and your loved one can work on together. For example, you can wash dishes while your loved one dries them, or you can wipe down the bathtub while your loved one wipes down the bathroom sink.

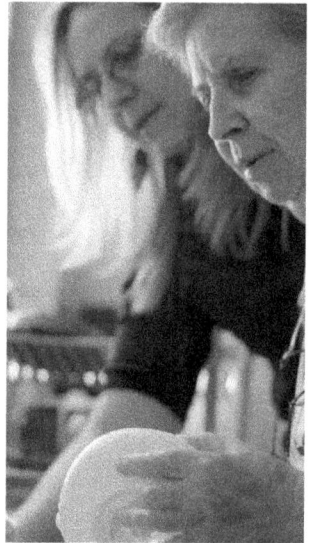

Credit: Orange Line Media

☑ Modify housekeeping tasks according to your loved one's abilities. For example, if your loved one struggles with balance, have them sit at the kitchen table while they wipe dishes or sit on the couch while they dust the coffee table.

☑ Store any harmful cleaning products or supplies in a locked cabinet when you are not around to supervise their use. Do not store bleach and ammonia close together, because mixing these chemicals can cause death from toxic fumes. Consider using nontoxic alternative cleaners where appropriate, such as vinegar and baking soda.

☑ Understand the difference between light and heavy cleaning. Light cleaning includes basic tasks that must be done regularly. Heavy cleaning includes more detailed, once-in-a-while tasks. Light cleaning tasks may be within your loved one's physical capabilities, but heavy cleaning tasks may not because these tasks often involve climbing, reaching, and moving furniture.

☑ Have realistic expectations of your loved one. Your loved one may be capable of performing some tasks independently or with your help but may also need to be reminded that the tasks must be done or how to do the tasks. Their abilities will change over time, and tasks they could perform last week may no longer be realistic.

☑ Have realistic expectations of yourself. You may not have the time or energy to perform housekeeping tasks with or for your loved one, particularly if you are maintaining your own home too. Understand your limitations, and consider hiring a homemaker or other service provider to assist with housekeeping tasks if you feel overwhelmed.

Using the Phone

Difficulty using the telephone often develops early in the progression of Alzheimer's disease; in fact, for some patients, it is one of the first signs of the disease. The telephone is an important link between your loved one and the outside world. As a result, trouble using the telephone can lead to safety concerns. This was certainly true of my father; I knew he was in trouble when I called him and he told me that he didn't know how to use the phone to call a friend.

Telephone problems can occur with both outgoing and incoming calls. Your loved one may have trouble remembering phone numbers, recognizing the digits on the phone, or identifying the phone, making it difficult for them to place outgoing calls. They may also forget that a ringing telephone must be answered or that they must say hello when picking up the phone. This can lead to confusion and panic, on your part as well as theirs. The questions below will help you determine whether your loved one is having difficulties using the phone.

Checklist: *Assessing whether your loved one needs help using the phone*

☑ Does your loved one know how to look up a phone number?

☑ Does your loved one recognize the digits on the phone keys?

☑ Does your loved one know how to push numbers in order?

☑ Does your loved one forget who they are trying to call while dialing?

☑ Does your loved one understand who you or others are over the telephone?

☑ Does your loved one frequently dial phone numbers incorrectly?

☑ Does your loved one call the same familiar number over and over?

☑ Does your loved one place calls at inappropriate times of day or night?

☑ Does your loved one let the phone ring without answering?

☑ Does your loved one answer the phone and say nothing?

☑ Does your loved one forget to hang up the phone at the end of a call?

☑ Does your loved one confuse the phone with other household items?

☑ Does your loved one respond favorably to scam phone calls or telemarketers?

Some phone issues are minor and relatively harmless, like attempting to answer the phone using the television remote. Others may be irritating or expensive, like repeatedly calling the same person in the middle of the night or accidentally making an international phone call. Still others can be downright frightening to you as a caregiver, like your loved one failing to answer your repeated phone calls. The checklist below offers some ideas for promoting effective phone use.

Checklist: *Techniques to help your loved one use the phone*

☑ Use phones with oversized buttons in a contrasting color to the phone base (e.g., black buttons on a white phone base) so the buttons are easy for your loved one to see. Place phones on tables of contrasting color (e.g., a white phone on a brown table) to make them more visible to your loved one.

☑ Post instructions for phone use near all telephones. Instructions should include information about dialing for outgoing calls and answering for incoming calls. They should also remind your loved one to hang up the phone at the end of the call.

☑ Keep emergency contact numbers in easy reach of all phones. Include a brief description or photo of the person or organization next to the number. Remember to include numbers for your loved one's doctor, the fire department, the police department, and poison control.

☑ If your loved one's phones have speed dial, program numbers for caregivers and emergency personnel. Make a list of the numbers in large font (e.g., 1 = daughter, 2 = police, etc.) and place it next to each phone.

☑ If your loved one struggles with speed dial, consider a photo phone. Numbers are programmed into the photo phone the same way they are programmed into speed dial, but the buttons hold small pictures. Your loved one simply presses the picture of the person they want to call rather than finding a name on a list and pressing a number.

☑ If your loved one is comfortable with cell phones, consider getting one with voice recognition dialing. This will enable your loved one to press a button and say the name of the person they want to call, and the phone will dial the saved number for them. Also, many cell phones can be tracked remotely via built-in GPS, making them easier to find than landline phones if your loved one misplaces the cell phone.

Credit: Ruslan Guzov

☑ Ask friends or family members who frequently call your loved one to identify themselves immediately when your loved one answers the phone. Encourage them to keep the calls brief; the lack of visual cues when talking on the phone can create confusion or agitation for individuals with Alzheimer's disease.

☑ Place a caller ID device on the phone. If your loved one fails to take phone messages or frequently does not answer the phone, reviewing the caller ID can alert you to important calls you might otherwise be unaware of, like doctor's appointment reminders.

☑ If your loved one is not able to answer incoming calls, provide your cell phone number to doctors and other service providers as a point of contact for your loved one. Encourage friends and family to call your cell phone if they wish to speak to your loved one. Alternatively, set up call forwarding so all calls go directly to your cell phone or use an answering machine to answer all calls.

☑ If your loved one frequently responds favorably to scam phone calls or telemarketers, set up the phone so it goes automatically to an answering system rather than ringing. Remind your loved one to never give out personal information over the phone, and ask them to consult you before making any financial decisions.

Transportation

A diagnosis of Alzheimer's disease does not automatically mean your loved one can no longer handle their own transportation. For some patients, driving is still an option for a period of time. Public transportation and walking may also be reasonable methods of getting around depending on where your loved one lives; these options work best if your loved one is already familiar with the transportation system or neighborhood.

Being aware of your loved one's abilities is especially important with transportation. You are responsible for the safety of your loved one, and you are also responsible for the safety of others on the road, bus, or sidewalk with your loved one. For these reasons, you must frequently assess whether getting around independently is still realistic for your loved one. No matter the mode of transportation your loved one is using, the questions below will assist you in determining whether they need help getting around.

Checklist: Assessing whether your loved one needs help with transportation

☑ Is your loved one able to recite their name and address?

☑ Does your loved one forget where they are going during trips?

☑ Does your loved one get lost on familiar routes?

☑ Can your loved one drive safely?

☑ Does your loved one recognize basic traffic signs?

☑ Does your loved one understand how to take public transportation?

☑ Can your loved one read a public transportation timetable?

☑ Does your loved one get off at the right stop when taking public transportation?

☑ Does your loved one remain on the sidewalk when walking?

☑ Does your loved one stop, look, and listen before crossing the street?

☑ Do traffic and traffic sounds disorient or agitate your loved one?

The best way to assess your loved one's transportation abilities is to make regular trips with them. If they still drive, ride along as a passenger; if they take the bus or walk, accompany them. When observing your loved one, remember not to judge their abilities based on a single incident. Running one stop sign or missing one bus stop doesn't mean they are incapable of venturing out alone, but it does mean you may need to observe their transportation habits more often. It may also be helpful to record your observations in a notebook.

Eventually, your loved one will no longer be able to travel through their community alone. At this point, you must be prepared to take away their keys, their bus pass, or their walking stick. Doing so is very difficult, but it is also necessary. The worst fight I ever had with my father was over driving and taking away his keys. I finally agreed with him that if he passed the driving test, I would let him drive. I then went home, printed a written driving test, and gave it to him. He returned it to me with only one question answered. I told him that I would send the test to the state to be graded, but he never mentioned it again, and neither did I. When the time comes for you to consider transportation issues, the checklist below offers suggestions for helping your loved one remain an independent traveler as long as possible.

Checklist: *Helping your loved one get around independently*

☑ Know when your loved one will be coming and going to and from errands, appointments, and other trips out of the house. Check in with them to make sure they arrive home safely.

☑ Get a medical ID bracelet for your loved one. The ID should include their name, their condition, and a contact number so you can be reached if your loved one becomes lost. Programs like MedicAlert® + Safe Return® also offer emergency response for Alzheimer's patients who become lost.

☑ Encourage your loved one to use the restroom before leaving the house. This will lessen the need to search for a bathroom while out and decrease the likelihood of accidents away from home.

☑ Purchase a prepaid gas card that can be used for filling up the car to simplify trips to the gas station if your loved one still drives.

☑ Purchase prepaid fare cards or tokens so your loved one does not have to worry about counting exact change if they use public transportation.

☑ Provide your loved one with a public transportation map that shows their common stops, including their home stop. Even if your loved one won't use the map, others who stop to help will find it useful.

Credit: Radu Razvan

☑ Provide a jacket with reflective features for your loved one to wear when walking. Many athletic clothing companies incorporate reflective elements into the designs of clothing made for runners. Glowing wristbands, light-up zipper pulls, and safety vests can also be purchased from retailers.

☑ Recruit family members and friends to help with transportation. This takes some of the transportation burden off of you and offers your loved one the chance to socialize with others. Make sure appointments or outings are scheduled at a time that works for the driver, and make the driver aware of your loved one's typical schedule and behaviors.

☑ Consider using a transportation service. Low- or no-cost options may be available through senior centers in your area. For-profit taxi services may also be an option. Make certain the driver understands your loved one's condition and is given explicit directions. If payment is required, try to make arrangements in advance.

Managing Money

Managing money is another IADL that becomes increasingly difficult for individuals with Alzheimer's disease. Early indicators that your loved one needs help with their money may involve more complex financial tasks, like filing tax returns or balancing the checkbook. As time goes on, more basic tasks like paying bills, using the ATM, or counting change will become a struggle. Knowing what's going on with your loved one's finances is essential because little issues can add up quickly, causing big financial problems for your loved one.

In addition to helping your loved one manage their money, you also need to safeguard them against financial exploitation. Businesses and individuals alike may prey on older adults using deception and questionable practices. Remember, too, that unscrupulous strangers may not be the only individuals looking to profit off of your loved one; family members often have means and opportunity for doing so. In my father's case, he gave away thousands of dollars to strangers who were preying on him. We reported it to the police, and because some of the scams originated overseas, we even reported it to federal agencies, but all to no avail. I had to have all of his mail forwarded to me and all his phone calls forwarded to my phone to put a stop to it. The questions below will help you assess whether your loved one needs help managing their money and protecting their finances against fraud.

Checklist: *Assessing if your loved one needs help managing money*

☑ Does my loved one struggle with performing basic mathematic calculations?

☑ Can my loved one recognize and count money correctly?

☑ Does my loved one pay bills on time and for the right amount?

☑ Does my loved one remember how to balance a checkbook?

☑ Does my loved one recognize financial scams?

☑ Does my loved one open bills or allow them to pile up unopened?

☑ Has my loved one made any unusual or expensive purchases or donations lately?

☑ Has my loved one made any large transactions or withdrawals?

☑ Has my loved one had unnecessary work done to their home?

☑ Has my loved one received past due notices or creditor calls?

☑ Has my loved one had utilities shut off for nonpayment?

It is generally wise to discuss your loved one's finances and devise a plan early in the progression of their disease, before they show signs of struggling with money management. Consider obtaining a durable power of attorney for finances, in which your loved one grants control of financial decisions to another person upon incapacitation. The document should be executed while your loved one can still understand and agree to the arrangement.

Even with a power of attorney for finances in place, remember that conversations about finances must be approached delicately. Your loved one may believe they are doing a fine job with their finances even though it is clear to you they are struggling. In addition, many people consider being in control of personal finances an important part of being independent. As a result, your loved one may be suspicious of your motives and resistant to your help managing their money. Gradually transitioning financial responsibilities from your loved one to yourself rather than simply taking over may help ease some their concerns. The checklist below offers a few suggestions to help you with this process.

Checklist: *Helping your loved one manage their money*

☑ Frame your assistance as a learning experience. Tell your loved one that you want to know more about managing finances and you'd like their help learning about it.

☑ Start small by helping with one or two tasks. Look for tasks your loved one has never enjoyed doing in the past, such as filing tax returns. Your loved one may be more willing to let go of these tasks.

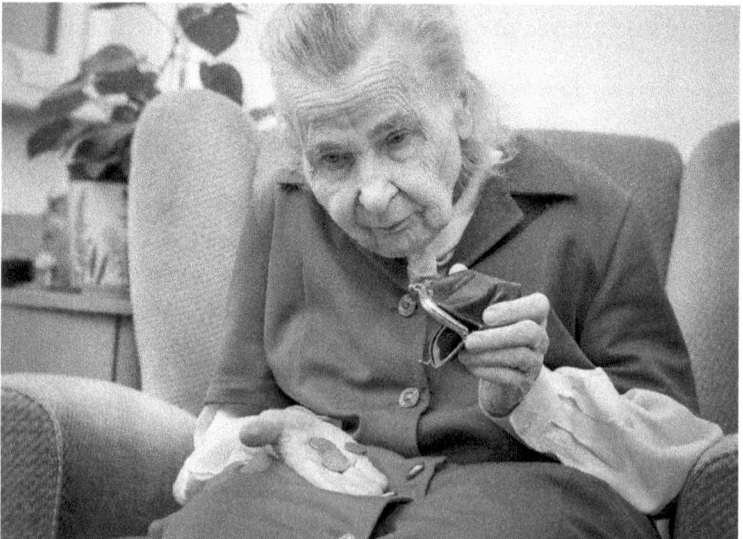

Credit: Alexander Raths

☑ Help your loved one go through their mail. Open bills and financial statements and read them together. Throw away solicitations from disreputable organizations or organizations that have no connection to your loved one.

☑ Set up online bill payments when possible. Walk through the payment process with your loved one each month, allowing them to do as much of it as they can on their own.

☑ Give your loved one small amounts of cash in small bills to have on hand to help them maintain independence and enable them to make small purchases.

☑ If your loved one insists on using checks, maintain a balance in their checking account that is only sufficient to cover their typical needs, then transfer the majority of funds to a savings or money market account. Alert the bank to the possibility of checks written to fraudulent businesses and have them notify you if your loved one's written checks seem out of character. Also make sure your loved one's checking account has overdraft protection to avoid overdraft fees.

☑ Give your loved one preloaded debit cards rather than credit cards or debit cards linked to their bank account. This will prevent overspending and limit the damage to your loved one's finances if the card is lost or stolen.

☑ If your loved one insists on keeping a credit card, cancel all cards except one. Ask the credit card company to minimize the credit limit on that card.

☑ Check the power of attorney requirements at your loved one's financial institutions. Many institutions require the completion of proprietary forms in addition to copies of the legal documents. These forms must be completed while your loved one is still considered competent to sign them.

☑ Review your loved one's financial data. Tax returns, investment portfolio reports, and bank statements all provide essential information. Go through any loan or credit agreements and Social Security and pension paperwork. This will help you get a sense of your loved one's current obligations and assets.

☑ Secure your loved one's important financial documents, such as mortgage information or deeds to property, automobile titles, and their will. If these items are in a safe deposit box, obtain a copy of the key or have your loved one remove them from the safe deposit box and put them in a secure location in their home.

☑ Request copies of your loved one's credit reports and monitor them for unusual activity. Such activity may indicate that your loved one has been a victim of fraud or had their identity stolen. Free annual credit reports are available from all three credit bureaus.

☑ Don't argue with your loved one over their finances. If they are resistant to your help or suggestions, drop the subject and come back to it later.

Taking Medicine

Older adults often take a variety of medications for chronic diseases or conditions. This can be a big challenge for individuals with Alzheimer's disease. Because of their deteriorating memory, your loved one may forget to take their medication or may take the wrong dose. They may also struggle with the special instructions that accompany certain medications, such as taking them with food or at certain times of day.

One of your responsibilities as a caregiver is to make sure your loved one takes the right dose of the right medication at the right time. Failure to do so can lead to medication-related problems that may include worsening of chronic conditions, accelerated cognitive impairment, and overdose. The questions below can help you assess whether your loved one may be struggling to take their medication correctly.

Checklist: *Assessing whether your loved one needs help with taking medicine*

☑ Does your loved one know the correct dosage for each of their medications?

☑ Does your loved one understand when medications must be taken?

☑ Is your loved one able to follow any special instructions that accompany medications?

☑ Does your loved one remember to fill prescriptions when needed?

☑ Does your loved one finish prescriptions too quickly?

☑ Does your loved one not finish prescriptions quickly enough?

☑ Can your loved one recognize different medications by their shape and color?

On average, older adults take four prescription medications each day. The more complex an older adult's medical conditions, the greater the number of prescription medications that person takes—and the more medications an individual takes, the greater the risk for medication-related problems. When you consider this in light of the changing cognitive abilities of your loved one with Alzheimer's disease, it is easy to understand why your involvement in their medication regimen is important.

The checklist below offers some suggestions for helping your loved one take their medication safely. Remember, while simple reminders and aids like pill organizers may be sufficient for helping your loved one in the early stages of Alzheimer's disease, your approach to and involvement with medication will change as time goes on.

Checklist: *Helping your loved one take medication safely*

☑ Maintain a list of all of your loved one's current medications, including prescriptions, over-the-counter medicines, and supplements. Write the name, purpose, and schedule for each medication on the list. Keep the list with you at all times and take it to all of your loved one's doctor appointments.

☑ Develop a medication routine for your loved one. Medications should be taken at the same time and in the same way each day, and in accordance with their written directions. When possible, pair medication administration with another activity, like a meal or going to bed.

☑ Supervise your loved one when they take their medication to ensure correct dosing on the correct schedule.

☑ Use a pill box organizer to maintain your loved one's medication schedule. Simple plastic organizers are available at most stores. Programmable electronic pill boxes are also available through some retailers.

☑ Provide clear, simple, step-by-step instructions to your loved one when taking medication.

Credit: jdwfoto

☑ Place medications in a locked cabinet or drawer until it is time to take them. Safely dispose of medications that are no longer necessary or have expired.

☑ If your loved one has difficulty swallowing pills, ask if a liquid formulation of the medicine is available. If not, ask whether the medication can be crushed. Always check before crushing medications as some may lose effectiveness or become harmful when crushed.

☑ Mix medications with soft foods like applesauce or ice cream if a physician indicates that it is safe to do so.

☑ Discuss potential side effects, allergies, and drug interactions with your loved one's doctor or pharmacist when new medications are prescribed and if you notice the development of any sudden, unusual changes in your loved one.

☑ If your loved one refuses to take their medication, don't force them. Stop and try again later. Talk with your loved one's doctor if medication refusal becomes problematic.

☑ If your loved one's medication schedule is complex, considering hiring a home health aide for an hour per day to supervise medication administration.

Other IADL

The IADL discussed earlier in this book are generally considered essential for individuals living independently in the community. Depending upon your loved one's beliefs, preferences, and lifelong habits, you may consider some other activities under the umbrella of IADL. These may include your loved one's ability to observe their customary religious practices or care for any pets living in their household. You should also assess your loved one's ability to respond appropriately in emergency situations. As with other IADL, abilities in these areas will change over time and should be regularly assessed.

Behavioral Challenges

In addition to changes in your loved one's ability to perform ADL and IADL, behavioral changes often accompany deteriorating cognitive function. Challenging behaviors can take many forms, but certain behaviors are common to people with Alzheimer's disease. Some behaviors—such as those related to memory and concentration—may be easier for you to understand than others—such as anger, aggression, and depression. This is especially true if your loved one's challenging behavior is at odds with their general temperament.

Behavioral changes can be troubling and hard to cope with as a caregiver, prompting feelings of confusion, embarrassment, irritation, or even fear. When your loved one's actions or words prompt these emotions, remember that you cannot change their behavior—only your reaction to it. Try to remain calm, assess what is causing the behavior, and change the environment or situation to help overcome the problem.

Knowing how to identify behavioral triggers will help you address challenging behaviors when they arise. Challenging behaviors may be triggered by something that upsets your loved one, by an inability to meet basic needs, or by restlessness and boredom. These behaviors may also be an attempt to communicate, particularly if your loved one struggles to do so verbally. The questions below will help you assess some general behavioral triggers; subsequent sections provide insight into specific behaviors.

Checklist: *Assessing possible behavioral triggers*

- ☑ Has anything happened in the last five or ten minutes to upset your loved one?

- ☑ Has your loved one recently experienced a change in their normal routine?

- ☑ Has your loved one been getting sufficient sleep and exercise?

- ☑ When did your loved one last eat or drink?

☑ Does your loved one appear to be in pain?

☑ Do your loved one's words or actions indicate that they are frightened of something?

☑ Do your loved one's words or actions suggest they are reliving an event from the past?

☑ Does your loved one show signs of being too hot or too cold, like sweating or shivering?

☑ Does your loved one show signs of boredom, like fidgeting or pacing?

☑ Does your loved one show signs of needing to use the bathroom or soiling their clothes?

☑ Is there sufficient light for your loved one to identify the objects or people in the room?

☑ Is there too much noise being made or too much action going on around your loved one?

☑ Have you been communicating anger, frustration, or other negative emotions to your loved one?

Memory Loss

Memory loss is one of the earliest signs of Alzheimer's disease and is the characteristic that many people most strongly associate with the disease. As a result, caregivers expect and anticipate various memory-related problems, such as misplacing things, forgetting appointments or recent events, and struggling to recognize people and places. In my father's case, he forgot the meaning of basic words. One time, he asked me who I was. When I told him that I was his daughter, he replied, "I don't know what the word daughter means." What can be surprising to many caregivers, however, is the way memory problems manifest themselves through behavior.

Memory loss affects each person differently, resulting in a range of unusual or challenging behaviors. These behaviors can often be categorized by type. For example, asking the same question over and over, calling the same phone number over and over, or putting on and taking off the same sweater over and over are different behaviors that are all categorized as repetitive. Repetitive behaviors may occur simply because your loved one does not remember having said or done them previously; they may also occur as a result of your loved one's efforts to maintain a sense of purpose or structure. The checklist below identifies some behaviors indicative of progressing memory loss.

Checklist: *Signs of progressing memory loss*

☑ Your loved one frequently repeats words or phrases.

☑ Your loved one frequently asks the same question.

☑ Your loved one repeatedly calls you or others on the phone, often at inappropriate times.

☑ Your loved one frequently repeats an action or series of actions.

☑ Your loved one can't remember where they have placed something.

☑ Your loved one hides things for safekeeping and later does not remember hiding them.

☑ Your loved one rummages through drawers or cabinets looking for missing items.

☑ Your loved one forgets important or regular appointments.

☑ Your loved one doesn't remember that someone visited the day before.

☑ Your loved one does not recognize someone they've known for years.

☑ Your loved one remembers the distant past better than the recent past.

☑ Your loved one believes they still have a job and regularly goes through the motions they previously carried out at work.

☑ Your loved one believes they are living in the past and mistakes you or others for a parent, sibling, or friend from the past.

☑ Your loved one frequently asks where they are and why they are there.

☑ Your loved one doesn't recognize their own home and frequently asks you to take them home.

☑ Your loved one is unable to perform ADL or IADL.

Memory loss can be frustrating for your loved one, particularly in the early stages of Alzheimer's disease. Your loved one's memory loss and the resultant behaviors may also be stressful to you as a caregiver. It is important for you to control these emotions around your loved one. Your stress will increase their stress, these feelings will make it harder for your loved one to remember, and their inability to remember will lead to more challenging behaviors. The checklist below offers some tips for coping with your loved one's memory loss and the unusual behaviors associated with it.

Checklist: *Coping with memory loss*

☑ Be tactful and patient with repeated questions. When possible, help your loved one find the answer on their own. For example, if they often ask you the time, direct their attention to the clock.

☑ Avoid mentioning an upcoming event until just before it takes place. This may lessen your loved one's anxiety about the event and result in fewer repeated questions about it.

☑ Direct your loved one's attention away from repeated phrases or actions through activity. Going for a walk, completing a basic household chore, or engaging in a simple creative activity may help.

☑ Engage your loved one in conversation about a repeated action. Often, such actions are related to an activity your loved one previously enjoyed. Talking about it offers an opportunity for your loved one to reminisce.

☑ Learn your loved one's hiding places so you can help locate lost or hidden items. Check hiding places regularly for perishable items that may spoil.

☑ Keep duplicates of your loved one's important items that are apt to get misplaced, like eyeglasses or wallets. If the original item cannot be located, "find" one of the replacements and give it to your loved one.

☑ Secure items that are important or irreplaceable, such as your purse or wallet, your keys, and any important documents that may be in the home.

☑ Create a "rummage box" for your loved one. Place an assortment of safe, interesting items in the box and encourage your loved one to go through the box rather than rummaging in cabinets or drawers.

☑ Use memory aids to help your loved one keep track of upcoming appointments. Write appointments on a large calendar or chart and use a red marker to cross off days as they occur.

☑ Create a "visitors log" to record guests who come to visit. Make a note of the day and time they visited and what they talked about with your loved one. Your loved one can refer back to this information to help remember their visitors.

☑ Look through photo albums containing pictures of family and friends, and talk about the photos with your loved one. Rather than asking your loved one if they remember someone in a photo, say things like, "There's your brother, Andrew. He always baked the most wonderful bread and served it with butter and jam."

☑ Use descriptive introductions when guests come to visit. Say something like, "Your friend John Williams from State University is here. You two were roommates when you lived in the dorms." Do not expect your loved one to recognize guests; doing so will make them feel "on the spot" and create stress.

☑ Accept your loved one's sense of time rather orienting them to the present. For example, play along if they believe they are a teenager and you are their best friend, provided that doing so does not endanger either of you.

☑ Avoid sharing distressing information with your loved one. For example, they may not remember that a parent or sibling has died and may ask about that person. Do not remind them that the person has died; instead, encourage your loved one to talk about the person and that period in their life.

☑ Reassure your loved one that they are safe, even if they do not recognize their current environment as home. Remind them that you love them and will take care of them.

Difficulty Concentrating

Individuals with Alzheimer's disease may also struggle with concentration. Disease-related changes to the brain make it difficult for these individuals to filter out environmental disruptions, affecting their ability to concentrate. During the early stages of Alzheimer's disease, difficulties are most noticeable with lengthy or complex tasks; over time, you may notice your loved one struggling to attend to even short, simple tasks.

Some behaviors associated with memory problems may also be associated with difficulty concentrating, such as repeating words, phrases, or questions. These may be most noticeable when engaging your loved one in conversation. Other behaviors include leaving tasks unfinished, giving up interests, and avoiding social situations. Frustration caused by the inability to concentrate may give rise to these behaviors; inability to remember what is being done and why may also cause them. The following checklist offers some additional indicators that your loved one may be struggling with concentration.

Checklist: *Signs your loved one is having difficulty concentrating*

☑ Your loved one is easily distracted by noise and other people.

☑ Your loved one has trouble following verbal or written instructions.

☑ Your loved one has trouble following familiar processes, like preparing a favorite recipe.

☑ Your loved one must restart tasks from the beginning after an interruption.

☑ Your loved one has given up a hobby that once occupied much of their time.

☑ Your loved one begins tasks but does not finish them.

☑ Your loved one has lost interest in social activities.

☑ Your loved one struggles to follow conversations, especially in group settings.

☑ Your loved one loses their train of thought while speaking.

☑ Your loved one jumps from topic to topic when speaking.

☑ Your loved one walks away or starts another activity in the middle of a conversation.

☑ Your loved one reads the same page of a book or magazine multiple times.

☑ Your loved one rarely watches an entire movie or TV show or finishes a book.

☑ Your loved one tends to fixate on one idea to the exclusion of everything else.

☑ Your loved one stares into space or seems vacant for long periods of time.

Individuals with concentration problems often benefit from simple changes in their approach to tasks, and the checklist below offers some tips for making these changes. Remember that your loved one's ability to concentrate may change from day to day, and your approach may need to change accordingly. Rest, exercise, and nutrition can all affect your loved one's abilities. Common illnesses unrelated to Alzheimer's disease—such as a cold or the flu—can also make concentration problems worse.

Checklist: *Coping with concentration problems*

☑ Allow plenty of time for tasks and try not to rush your loved one.

☑ Complete complex or multistep tasks during the time of day when your loved one is most rested, most alert, and at their best.

Credit: Budimir Jevtic

☑ Give your loved one directions one step at a time. For example, if you need them to set the table, ask them to put out the placemats; when that is done, ask them to put out the plates; when that is done, ask them to put out the forks.

☑ Reduce distractions to help your loved one concentrate. Turn off the TV or radio, clear clutter from the area, and move to a place where you will not be interrupted by others.

☑ Make sure your loved one can see and hear adequately. If your loved one normally wears glasses or hearing aids, make sure they are wearing those items. Provide adequate lighting, and speak slowly and clearly.

☑ Focus on activities your loved one enjoys. They may be able to concentrate on these activities longer than those they dislike or have no strong feelings about.

☑ Watch for signs that your loved one is distracted or uncertain about what to do, then redirect their attention or provide the next step in the process.

☑ If your loved one becomes frustrated with a task, set it aside and come back to it later.

☑ Play movies or shows for your loved one that move slowly, have simple plots, and don't have a lot of loud music or special effects. Consider using videos rather than watching shows live to eliminate the distraction of commercials. Ball games or other programs that can be enjoyed with minimal attention may also be appropriate.

☑ Provide books, magazines, or newspapers with large print. Larger print means fewer words per page, and fewer words mean fewer visual distractions.

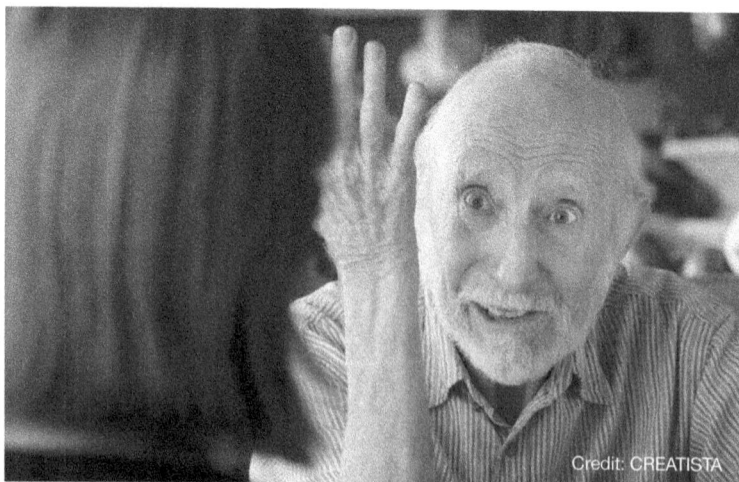

☑ Discuss medication side effects with your loved one's pharmacist or physician. Difficulty concentrating is a side effect of some drugs, and changes to your loved one's prescriptions may improve their ability to concentrate.

Anger

Memory loss, concentration problems, and many of the other changes that occur with Alzheimer's disease can be difficult for your loved one to contend with, prompting feelings of stress, frustration, and anger. Innocuous tasks or simple requests may result in angry outbursts by your loved one. Such outbursts may be out of character for your loved one and can be jarring or frightening to you as a caregiver. Though it can be difficult, you should try to apply a problem-solving approach to your loved one's anger and the associated behaviors.

Causes of anger and angry outbursts may be biological, social, or psychological in nature. Individuals with Alzheimer's disease experience pain, loneliness, and frustration just like everyone else, but they may lack the capacity to understand and cope with these emotions. The following checklist offers some examples of biological, social, and psychological issues that may lead to anger in your loved one.

Checklist: Identifying causes of anger

☑ Your loved one is sick, in pain, or uncomfortable.

☑ Your loved one is tired, hungry, or thirsty.

☑ Your loved one struggles to complete basic tasks on their own.

☑ Your loved one has vision or hearing problems that lead to misperceptions.

☑ Your loved one is bored or lonely.

☑ Your loved one misinterprets your actions, words, or intentions.

☑ Your loved one believes you are a stranger rather than a trusted caregiver.

☑ Your loved one feels they are not being listened to or are being left out of decisions.

☑ Your loved one does not recognize their environment as their home.

☑ Your loved one's regular routine has been disrupted.

☑ Your loved one is overstimulated by noise or people in their environment.

Even when you carefully observe your loved one's biological, social, and psychological states and attempt to meet their needs appropriately, angry episodes may still occur from time to time. When they do, your reaction to the situation will dictate how long these episodes last and to what level they escalate. The following checklist provides some ideas for handling your loved one's anger and anger-related behaviors.

Checklist: *How to deal with anger*

☑ Do not take your loved one's anger personally. Remember that your loved one is responding to needs that aren't being met or emotions they do not understand; they are not trying to scare or intimidate you.

☑ Observe your loved one's body language and facial expressions for clues to what is causing their anger. Watch for signs that they are frightened or in pain.

☑ Remain calm and offer gentle reassurance to your loved one. Raising your voice or being confrontational will only escalate the situation.

☑ Do not try to discuss your loved one's anger in the moment. They may lack the ability to reflect on their behavior and the ability to learn how to control it, and discussion will only increase their agitation.

☑ Maintain physical distance during angry outbursts. Initiating physical contact may prompt your loved one to become physically violent.

☑ If your loved one is in a safe location, give them space to be angry alone. Step back and monitor their behavior from a safe distance.

☑ Consider whether the activity that prompted the anger must be done immediately. If it can wait, let it go and return to it later.

☑ Look for patterns in your loved one's anger to identify activities or topics that lead to outbursts. Consider whether outbursts occur at specific times of day.

☑ Engage your loved one in a favorite activity during the times of day when they tend to experience anger. Play music, have a conversation, or take a walk to ease the feelings that lead to anger. Avoid activities that prompt angry episodes at such times of day.

☑ Ask another trusted caregiver to assist you if you must engage your loved one in an activity that tends to lead to angry outbursts.

☑ Try to carry on normally once an outburst has ended. Don't punish your loved one for their behavior, and acknowledge any sadness or distress they feel after the incident.

☑ Discuss angry incidents with others. Join a support group for caregivers, talk to other caregivers, or confide in a friend. Be careful not to have such discussions in front of or within earshot of your loved one.

Aggression

More than one-third of individuals with Alzheimer's disease occasionally exhibit aggressive behavior. For some individuals, anger and angry episodes may lead to aggression. For others, aggression may occur without warning, catching caregivers off guard. Aggressive behavior may be linked to your loved one's personality prior to their diagnosis. It is not uncommon, however, for people who have never shown aggression to exhibit aggressive behaviors in the moderate and severe stages of Alzheimer's disease.

Aggressive behavior may be physical or verbal. Physical aggression includes hitting, pinching, throwing, scratching, hair pulling, and biting. Verbal aggression includes screaming, shouting, swearing, and making threats. Some of these characteristics are common to both angry outbursts and verbal aggression; a key difference is in the way the screaming and shouting are directed. In an angry outburst, the shouting may not be directed at a specific person, while in an aggressive episode, it is most likely directed at a caregiver or other nearby individual.

Aggressive behaviors are caused by disease-related changes in the brain that affect an individual's inhibitions and sense of what is socially appropriate. As a result, in frightening, threatening, or uncomfortable situations, the individual with Alzheimer's disease may lash out because they do not realize it is inappropriate to do so. For individuals who struggle to communicate, aggression may be a means of expressing what they are feeling.

Aggression is caused by many of the previously identified biological, social, and psychological circumstances that lead to angry outbursts. Addressing those circumstances may reduce the likelihood of an aggressive episode. If aggressive episodes do occur, it is important to remain calm and try to reassure your loved one. It is also essential to consider your own safety. The checklist below offers some tips for dealing with aggressive behavior.

Checklist: *How to deal with aggression*

☑ Don't take your loved one's aggression personally. While their words or actions may be directed at you, they are not meant as a personal attack. You are the one who is there in the moment, so they lash out at you.

- [✓] Try not to show fear, alarm, or anxiety. Doing so may increase your loved one's agitation. This may be especially difficult if aggression is out of character for your loved one or if the episode started unexpectedly.

- [✓] Maintain eye contact with your loved one and calmly explain who you are and why you are there. Let them know you are listening and encourage them to talk to you.

- [✓] Do not shout or talk over your loved one. Use calm, reassuring tones and neutral language.

- [✓] Do not attempt to restrain your loved one or initiate physical contact. Doing so may be misinterpreted as threatening behavior, which will increase their aggression and cause them to fight harder.

- [✓] Maintain your distance and keep out of your loved one's arms' reach if they tend to hit or push during aggressive episodes.

- [✓] Remove heavy and breakable items from living areas if your loved one tends to throw things during aggressive episodes.

- [✓] Step out of the room if you feel yourself becoming agitated or if you fear for your safety during an aggressive episode.

- [✓] If your loved one cannot be calmed down or if you feel increasingly threatened by their behavior, call for help.

Credit: Volodymyr Baleha

☑   After an aggressive episode, focus on your loved one and not on their behavior. They may not remember what happened, and discussing it or punishing them for it may cause them to become confused or upset.

☑   Report aggressive episodes to your loved one's doctor. Depending upon the frequency and intensity of such episodes, the doctor may prescribe an antipsychotic medication to control the aggression.

☑   If aggression worsens or is unmanageable, consider whether it is time to move your loved one to a full-time care facility.

Psychosis

Behavioral changes in your loved one with Alzheimer's disease may also be the result of psychosis, which is broadly defined as difficulty determining whether something is real or imagined. Psychosis affects as many as 50% of individuals with Alzheimer's disease over the course of the disease. Individuals who have previously been diagnosed with psychiatric disorders are more likely than others to experience psychosis. In addition, patients experiencing hallucinations or delusions are more likely to exhibit aggressive behaviors. Psychotic episodes typically occur during the moderate and severe stages of Alzheimer's disease and can lead to further deterioration of your loved one's cognitive abilities.

In some cases, you may have difficulty determining whether your loved one is exhibiting signs of confusion or signs of psychosis. Confusion manifests as trouble orienting to time, place, or people and can often be relieved through gentle reminders to your loved one. Psychosis, on the other hand, typically manifests in one of two ways. The first is delusions, which are false beliefs that cannot be changed, even when you can prove they are not true. The second is hallucinations, which involve perceiving through the senses things that are not actually there. The following checklist offers some additional information about the symptoms of psychosis.

Checklist: Signs your loved one is experiencing a psychotic episode

☑ Your loved one has delusions (i.e., they believe something is true despite evidence to the contrary). For example, your loved one may believe they are being threatened by a "stranger," even if that stranger is their own child.

☑ Your loved one seems paranoid (i.e., they hold the false belief that someone is trying to harm them). For example, your loved one may believe that someone is stealing from them, hiding things from them, or is "out to get" them.

☑ Your loved one is suspicious of family, friends, and neighbors and makes accusations against them. For example, your loved one may accuse their partner of being unfaithful.

☑ Your loved one develops a fear of abandonment. They may begin to follow you and other caregivers around and frequently call out to you if they cannot see you.

☑ Your loved one has hallucinations (i.e., they experience something through the senses that is not real). Typically, hallucinations are visual or auditory and cause your loved one to see or hear things that are not actually there, though other senses such as taste or smell may also be impacted.

☑ Your loved one "sees" friends, parents, spouses, or pets who have died. They may talk to these individuals and be able to describe them to you in detail.

The symptoms associated with psychosis may be frightening to you as a caregiver; try to remember, though, that they are also frightening to your loved one. As with anger, aggression, and other behavioral issues, the best thing you can do during a psychotic episode is to remain calm and try to be supportive of your loved one. The checklist below offers a few ideas for handling psychotic episodes.

Checklist: *How to deal with a psychotic episode*

☑ Don't argue with your loved one about what is fact and what is fantasy. Remember that their reality is different from yours.

☑ Listen to the emotional cues in what your loved one is saying, even if the content is delusional. Respond to those emotions in calm, supportive ways.

☑ Comfort and calm your loved one using gentle, soothing touch like a hand or shoulder massage; by playing relaxing music; or by offering familiar personal items like a favorite blanket or soft toy.

☑ Encourage your loved one to talk about their symptoms. For example, if your loved one is experiencing a visual hallucination, it may be reassuring for them to discuss it with you. If the hallucination is unpleasant, let your loved one know you cannot see it but you will keep them safe.

☑ If you must ask questions of your loved one during an episode, ask closed-ended questions that require a yes-or-no answer ("Would you like a glass of water?") rather than open-ended questions ("What would you like to drink?").

☑ Distract your loved one with a favorite activity, a light snack, or a short walk.

☑ Avoid letting your loved one watch violent movies or television shows, as they can contribute to paranoia and delusions.

☑ Search for "hidden" or "stolen" items regularly. Check your loved one's typical hiding places and other places where items tend to be misplaced. Place found items where your loved one will see them but don't make a big show of having found them, because doing so may make your loved one feel you are questioning their delusions.

☑ Have your loved one's vision and hearing checked, and ensure they wear glasses or hearing aids if necessary. Problems with sight and hearing can contribute to hallucinations.

☑ Consult your loved one's physician about available medications and non-drug interventions that may lessen the likelihood of psychotic episodes.

Depression

Depression is common among individuals with Alzheimer's disease, though diagnosis can be difficult given that the two conditions share a number of symptoms. The cognitive impairment experienced by Alzheimer's patients further complicates diagnosis, as individuals may lack the capacity to express their feelings of sadness and hopelessness. An estimated 40% to 50% of Alzheimer's patients experience depressive symptoms.

Depression often develops during the mild and moderate stages of Alzheimer's disease and may be less severe than depression among people who do not suffer from the disease. Symptoms tend to come and go, and depressive episodes tend to have a shorter duration than in individuals who have not been diagnosed with Alzheimer's disease. The following list identifies indicators that your loved one may be experiencing depression.

Checklist: Signs your loved one is depressed

☑ Your loved one is sad, hopeless, discouraged, or tearful.

☑ Your loved one is experiencing decreased pleasure or enjoyment from typical activities.

☑ Your loved one is socially isolated or withdrawn from social situations and other people.

☑ Your loved one has experienced a dramatic loss or increase in appetite that is unrelated to other conditions.

☑ Your loved one is either sleeping much more or much less than is typical.

☑ Your loved one is irritable or agitated more than is typical.

☑ Your loved one complains of fatigue or a loss of energy or appears lethargic.

☑ Your loved one has recurrent thoughts of death and has talked about or attempted suicide.

☑ Your loved one expresses feelings of low self-esteem, worthlessness, or guilt.

☑ Your loved one complains of aches and pains that have no apparent physical cause and are not tied to any medical condition.

☑ Your loved one has experienced a sudden, dramatic change in cognitive function.

Credit: Nadino

Schedule an appointment with your loved one's doctor if you suspect your loved one may be experiencing depression. Depending upon the doctor's area of expertise, they may conduct a thorough physical and psychological evaluation of your loved one, or they may refer your loved one to a geriatric psychiatrist for assessment. Geriatric psychiatrists specialize in recognizing and treating depression in older adults and are well-versed in the guidelines established by the National Institute of Mental Health for diagnosing depression in individuals with Alzheimer's disease.

Treatment for depression usually involves a combination of medicine, counseling, and activities that help individuals reconnect with people and things that bring them joy. The list below offers some suggestions for supporting a loved one who is experiencing depression.

Checklist: *Supporting your loved one with depression*

☑ Encourage your loved one to join a support group or see a counselor if they are in the mild stage of Alzheimer's disease. Talking with others who are aware of their Alzheimer's diagnosis and experiencing the sadness and frustration associated with it can help your loved one realize they are not alone.

☑ Maintain a routine in which your loved one sleeps, eats, exercises, and performs hygiene tasks at the same time each day. The routine should take your loved one's best times of day into account and block these times out for difficult or stressful tasks.

☑ Engage your loved one in their favorite activities as often as possible. Invite friends or family to join in the activities with you and your loved one.

☑ Exercise regularly with your loved one. Morning is an especially good time to take a walk or enjoy other light aerobic exercise.

☑ Engage your loved one in family activities as much as possible. Doing so will remind them that they are loved and appreciated by the family and that they can still contribute in meaningful ways.

☑ Maintain a calm, relaxing environment for your loved one, and limit distractions as much as possible. Overstimulation can worsen depressive symptoms.

☑ Review your loved one's medications with their physician, and ask whether depressive symptoms are a potential side effect of any medications.

☑ Stay positive. Offer support and praise to your loved one when appropriate and encouragement when necessary.

Other Behavioral Challenges

The challenges discussed previously are among those most commonly seen in individuals with Alzheimer's disease, but other unusual, difficult behaviors may also develop. In addition, the behavior of your loved one is likely to change as their illness progresses. The list below offers some additional examples of behavioral challenges your loved one may experience.

Checklist: Other behavioral changes that may occur with Alzheimer's disease

☑ Swearing

☑ Spitting

☑ Impulsiveness

☑ Loss of inhibitions

☑ Sexual harassment

☑ Loss of interest in former pleasures

☑ Social withdrawal

☑ Hoarding

☑ Shouting or screaming

☑ Pacing

No matter the behavior your loved one exhibits, try to remember it is not a result of their feelings toward you. Rather, it is a result of their illness and something that is beyond their control.

Sleep

Along with the challenges associated with ADL, IADL, and behavior, many individuals with Alzheimer's disease experience problems related to sleep. Researchers believe that sleep alterations in Alzheimer's disease are linked to the changes in the brain that produce memory and behavior issues. These changes affect what is known as the sleep/wake cycle, or the typical pattern of sleeping for about eight hours at night and being awake for about 16 hours during the day. Sleep problems may include trouble sleeping at night, nighttime wandering, and agitation or "sundowning."

The sleep changes experienced by people with Alzheimer's disease vary with disease progression. During mild Alzheimer's disease, individuals may sleep more than usual. In moderate and severe Alzheimer's disease, individuals may take multiple naps during the day and frequently wake during the night. In some cases, the sleep pattern may be completely reversed, with the individual doing all of their sleeping during the day and remaining awake all night. As Alzheimer's disease progresses, individuals rarely sleep for long periods, either at night or during the day.

Lack of sleep has negative cognitive effects on all people, including problems with memory, concentration, and alertness. For individuals diagnosed with Alzheimer's disease, these effects compound disease-related problems with cognition. Lack of sleep can also lead to increased behavioral challenges. The questions below will help you assess whether your loved one is having difficulty sleeping.

Checklist: Assessing whether your loved one is having difficulty sleeping

☑ Does your loved one sleep in later or wake up earlier than is typical in the mornings?

☑ Is your loved one very disoriented upon waking?

☑ Is your loved one's bedding twisted or pulled from the bed in the morning?

☑ Does your loved one seem drowsy during the day or take frequent short naps?

☑ Do you hear your loved one wake often or toss and turn during the night?

☑ Does your loved one cry or call out during the night?

☑ Has your loved one experienced sudden changes in cognitive abilities or behavior?

☑ Is your loved one prone to mood swings or anger late in the day?

☑ Does your loved one have increased difficulty with hand-eye coordination?

☑ Is your loved one prone to minor illnesses such as the common cold?

Sleep problems may be treated medically, nonmedically, or using a combination of medical and nonmedical techniques. Research suggests that sleep medications are generally not effective for older adults, and the National Institutes of Health encourage the use of non-drug treatment for sleep changes associated with Alzheimer's disease. Nonmedical techniques typically focus on providing a good sleep environment; sometimes this is referred to as promoting "good sleep hygiene." Sleep environment involves the sleeping area and routines that you and your loved one observe at bedtime. It also involves actions that can be taken throughout the day to improve the quality of your loved one's sleep. The following list offers some tips for creating a good sleep environment.

Checklist: Providing a good sleep environment

☑ Maintain a comfortable temperature in your loved one's bedroom. Watch for signs that your loved one is too hot or too cold and adjust the thermostat accordingly.

☑ Install a nightlight in your loved one's bedroom and make sure your loved one has any "security object" they like to sleep with. This may be a special pillow, blanket, or soft toy. Soft music or white noise machines may also be helpful.

☑ Place heavy shades or "blackout curtains" on the windows in your loved one's room. These will help block out nighttime light from streetlamps, headlights, and neighboring homes. This will also reduce the appearance of shadows in the room, which can frighten or disorient your loved one.

☑ Place a large display clock next to the bed. The clock should clearly indicate a.m. and p.m. or indicate night and day in some other easy-to-understand way.

☑ Encourage your loved one to use the bathroom right before getting in bed to decrease the need to get up and use the bathroom during the night. Consider putting a commode next to the bed to limit the need to get up.

☑ Allow your loved one to sleep in their clothes if they are resistant to putting on pajamas, particularly if they grow agitated about it.

☑ If your loved one struggles to fall asleep or tends to see or hear things that aren't there while dozing off, consider sitting with them until they fall asleep.

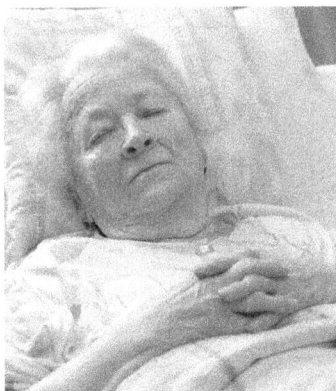

Credit: Volodymyr Baleha

☑ If your loved one wakes during the night, encourage them to move to a chair or couch until they feel sleepy. It may be helpful to give them a task such as folding laundry or reading during such periods of wakefulness, but avoid turning on the television.

☑ Maintain a regular schedule for going to bed and getting up for your loved one. It may also be helpful if meals are served at regular times each day.

☑ Avoid large meals in the evening. Serve a large meal at lunchtime and keep the evening meal small and simple. Avoid serving foods with a high sugar content with the evening meal.

☑ Limit your loved one's exposure to alcohol, caffeine, and nicotine, as these can impact the ability to sleep.

☑ Regularly expose your loved one to morning sunlight. Take a walk outside, sit on the porch, or simply open the blinds and allow the sun into the home.

☑ Avoid glaring or flashing lights in the evening as bedtime approaches. Light should be soft but adequate for your loved one to see their surroundings clearly.

☑ Engage in regular daily exercise with your loved one, but try to avoid doing so within four hours of bedtime.

☑ Manage your loved one's daytime sleep. Try to keep naps short and during the early and middle parts of the day. Encourage your loved one to nap on the couch or recliner rather than in bed.

☑ Ask your loved one's doctor to assess your loved one for underlying conditions that might interfere with sleep. Depression, pain, restless legs syndrome (a tingling sensation in the legs that causes an urge to move the legs), and sleep apnea (brief, frequent periods during which people stop breathing at night) can all contribute to sleep disruptions.

Although a good sleep environment can help your loved one get the sleep they need, it is not a guarantee of a good night's rest. Nighttime wakefulness is common among individuals with Alzheimer's disease, and estimates suggest that individuals with the disease may spend as much as 40% of the night awake. During these wakeful periods, some individuals are prone to wandering. Wandering spells not only prevent your loved one from getting they rest they need, but they are potentially dangerous. In addition, hearing your loved one wake and wander, or fearing that your loved one may wander, negatively affects your sleep. The checklist below offers some tips for preventing nighttime wandering and creating a safer environment if your loved one does attempt to wander.

Checklist: *How to prevent wandering at night*

☑ Install a peephole in your loved one's bedroom door that allows you to check on them without disturbing them.

☑ Place a baby monitor in your loved one's bedroom so you can hear if they get up during the night. Some monitors include a video display that will enable you to see as well as hear your loved one.

☑ Make a safe area for your loved one to walk or pace within their bedroom. Remove rugs, clutter, and furniture that present tripping hazards. Install a nightlight to help your loved one see where they are going.

☑ Paint the door and walls of your loved one's room the same color to camouflage the door and discourage your loved one from opening it and wandering the rest of the house.

☑ Place nightlights or glow-in-the dark tape along the path from your loved one's bedroom to the bathroom. This will help prevent your loved one from getting lost and wandering on their way to the bathroom. Remove any rugs or tripping hazards from the path.

☑ Install door sensors or motion detectors to alert you when your loved one is up and moving about the house.

☑ Close and secure doors to rooms or parts of the house that may be unsafe for your loved one. Restrict access to stairwells using tall safety gates, and make certain all windows and exterior doors are locked. If necessary, mount secondary locks low on exterior doors so they are out of your loved one's line of sight.

☑ Post "Stop" or "Keep out" signs on exterior doors or doors leading to potentially dangerous areas of the house.

☑ Replace finger-turn deadbolts and door locks on exterior doors with keyed deadbolts and door locks. In order to open this type of lock, a key must be inserted and turned in the lock whether on the inside or on the outside.

☑ Place baby safety covers on doorknobs leading to potentially dangerous areas of the house. In order to open a knob with the cover on it, the cover must be squeezed in the correct spot on either side. If it is not, it will simply spin around on the knob.

☑ Install shatterproof glass or plexiglass in windows and doors.

☑ Consider hiring a companion or nurse to come during the nighttime if your loved one wanders.

Sundowning

Closely tied to sleep problems is "sundowning," or a set of behaviors characterized by increased agitation, aggression, and confusion occurring late in the day and into the night. Sundowning usually occurs in moderate- and severe-stage Alzheimer's disease and may continue for several months. In some individuals, sundowning leads to pacing and wandering.

Studies suggest that up to 20% of individuals with Alzheimer's disease experience some type of increased anxiety and agitation late in the day. A major cause is shifts in the body's circadian rhythms, or the internal clock that controls the cycling of body temperature, metabolism, wakefulness, and sleep. Fatigue, poor lighting, and increased shadows also contribute. The following list offers some additional information about sundowning.

Checklist: *Basics about sundowning*

☑   Sundowning occurs when your loved one becomes confused or agitated around sunset (late afternoon or early evening).

☑   Physical and mental exhaustion at the end of the day may cause your loved one to sundown, as may changes in blood sugar or decreased blood pressure after evening meals.

☑   Diabetes, vision problems, or impaired hearing may make your loved one more susceptible to sundowning.

☑   Seasonal changes or time changes associated with Daylight Saving Time can worsen agitation and anxiety in the evening, causing sundowning in individuals who have not experienced it in the past.

☑   Problems separating dreams from reality can create disorientation that leads to sundowning.

☑   Attention span and concentration may become noticeably decreased during sundowning episodes, and impulsiveness may increase.

☑   Anxiety related to "going home" and other end-of-day tasks that were important in the past (such as picking up children from school) may increase.

☑   Individuals experiencing sundowning may start to shadow you, following you around and mimicking your behaviors.

☑   In some cases, individuals may lose full language abilities during sundowning episodes.

As with behavioral challenges, individuals with Alzheimer's disease have different triggers for sundowning, and it can be difficult to identify these triggers when sundowning episodes first occur.

It may be helpful to maintain a journal of your loved one's daily activities, environment, and behaviors until you identify their triggers. Common triggers include changes in the light that create shadows that appear threatening and increased hunger as evening mealtime approaches. Remember to reflect on your own behavior and nonverbal cues when exploring your loved one's triggers; your exhaustion at the end of the day may translate into body language that negatively impacts your loved one.

Even when you have identified your loved one's triggers and managed them appropriately, your loved one may still sundown. The checklist below offers some suggestions to help you prepare for sundowning episodes and handle them when they occur.

Checklist: *How to deal with sundowning*

☑ Establish a regular routine for sleeping, waking, activities, and meals.

☑ Place a full-spectrum fluorescent lamp (over 2,500 lux) near your loved one (within 1 yard) for a couple hours in the morning to reset their internal clock.

☑ Draw the curtains in the evening so your loved one does not see the sky change from light to dark.

☑ Maintain appropriate lighting in the evenings. Lighting should be bright enough so your loved one can see objects and people clearly, but not so bright that it causes overstimulation.

☑ Explain imagined images to your loved one to make them less threatening. For example, if shadows are creating threatening images, demonstrate that they are only shadows.

☑ If your loved one is agitated because of hunger, offer them a light snack or a drink until a meal is ready.

☑ Reduce background noise and plan quiet, relaxing activities that are meaningful to your loved one in the evenings. Limit television viewing during this time.

Credit: Goodluz

☑ Use techniques to help your loved one relax, such as playing soothing music, engaging in gentle touching (e.g., holding hands, stroking an arm), or handling familiar objects.

☑ Avoid taking your loved one to unfamiliar places late in the day. If you must leave the house during their typical sundowning time, bring familiar items like photographs or personal objects along to create some familiarity for your loved one.

☑ Remain calm with your loved one. Use soothing tones when speaking with your loved one, even if they are yelling. Reassure them that everything and everyone is safe.

☑ Discuss your loved one's sundowning with their physician. A physical exam may help determine whether a physical condition is causing pain or discomfort that may contribute to sundowning episodes.

Making Time to Care for Your Loved One

Caring for a loved one with Alzheimer's disease is a big commitment that grows as time goes on. Estimates suggest that caregivers spend an average of about 22 hours per week caring for their loved ones; this translates to roughly 1,140 hours of care per year. In the mild stage of Alzheimer's disease, these numbers could be less; in the moderate and severe stages, they could be more. No matter the stage of the disease, caring for your loved one is a balancing act involving your time and your obligations to work and family.

Work Life

The majority of Alzheimer's caregivers work outside of the home in addition to caring for their loved one, and the commitment to care has major effects on their work life. Fifty-four percent of working caregivers report going in late in the mornings, leaving early in the afternoons, or taking time off to care for their loved one, with 15% taking a leave of absence to engage in care activities. The federal Family and Medical Leave Act of 1993 (FMLA) offers employees up to 12 weeks of excused time off from work each year for serious health conditions. Under FMLA, Alzheimer's disease is considered a permanent or long-term condition, and employees may take FMLA leave to care for a parent or spouse with the disease. The following checklist outlines some of the basics of FMLA and may help you determine whether you are eligible for leave under the act.

Checklist: *FMLA Basics*

☑ Leave guaranteed by FMLA is unpaid, and it is at the employer's discretion whether benefits and pay will be provided while the employee is on leave.

☑ Employees must have worked at their company for more than 12 months and must have worked at least 1,250 hours during the previous year to be eligible for leave.

☑ Employees must provide a complete medical certification, which is a form that must be completed by the employee and a doctor providing details about the care situation. The certification must be returned within 15 days of receipt.

☑ Employees must complete a notification form letting employers know when leave will be taken. The notification must be submitted within two days of a leave request.

☑ Employers are responsible for providing certification, notification, and other necessary forms to employees who express a need for leave. Employers may include in-house paperwork and notifications in addition to those required by the government.

☑ Leave taken under FMLA may be continuous (the employee is absent for more than three consecutive business days), intermittent (the employee takes time off in separate hourly, daily, or weekly increments), or reduced schedule (the employee reduces the amount of hours worked per day or per week).

☑ Employees must be allowed to resume their former position upon their return from leave. If the employee can no longer perform that position, they must be provided with a comparable alternative position.

☑ Companies with fewer than 50 employees within 75 miles of the worksite are not required to provide FMLA leave to employees.

Leave under FMLA can be very helpful to caregivers, but the effects of caregiving on work extend beyond the need for time off. Over the long term, it may be necessary to permanently change your work schedule or opt for less-demanding job responsibilities. Leave, schedule changes, and responsibility changes all have financial consequences that must be considered as well.

Family Life

In addition to its effects on work life, making a care commitment to a loved one with Alzheimer's disease impacts your time and attention for your family. Essentially, committing yourself to care means you are committing your family as well. About 30% of

Alzheimer's disease and dementia caregivers are also parents to children under 18, and many more are parents to adult children. Caregivers with young children must find appropriate ways to meet the needs of their loved ones and their little ones. Often, this means explaining their loved one's condition to their children and finding ways to enlist their children in helping with care. This help may come in the form of small chores, increased independence with things like getting dressed or brushing teeth, or spending time with and entertaining your loved one. Adult children may be willing to take on larger-scale chores and home repairs, transport your loved one to and from appointments, and provide care to your loved one on the days when you need a break.

Spouses or long-term partners may also be willing and able to provide assistance with caregiving duties (assuming your loved one with Alzheimer's disease is not your spouse or partner). Keep in mind, however, that spouses and partners are affected by many of the same work issues that impact your ability to provide care. In addition, they may have their own caregiving responsibilities for sick or elderly loved ones.

Even when family members are involved in caring for your loved one, it is important to make time for them away from the care setting. It is easy to make a loved one with Alzheimer's disease the center of attention, but this can leave other family members feeling overlooked. Sitting down with your family and talking about care responsibilities and how they are affecting your relationships can help. Scheduling family events away from your loved one is also important. Even if you are committed to providing full care to your loved one yourself, it is wise to have another reliable caregiver—either paid or unpaid—who you can call upon when family obligations necessitate time away from your loved one.

Taking time away from your caregiving responsibilities to spend time with your family may also have positive benefits for you. Caring for a loved one with Alzheimer's disease takes a toll on both your mental and physical health, and enjoying a meal with your family or attending a school event with your child will yield positive benefits to your well-being.

Conclusion

Basic daily tasks essential to maintaining health and living independently will pose greater challenges to your loved one with Alzheimer's disease as their illness progresses. As a caregiver, you will be responsible for helping your loved one complete these tasks. This can be challenging because it signals the end of your loved one's independence. Given the personal nature of many of these tasks, this can also be stressful or embarrassing for both you and your loved one. To further compound the situation, behavioral changes may accompany changes in your loved one's ability to complete ADL and IADL independently.

No matter the challenges you and your loved one face as these changes occur, it is important to stay calm and remember that these changes are part of the illness and are not reflective of the way your loved one feels about you. It is also important to strike the right balance when caring for your loved one. This balance will depend upon your work and family obligations as well as your caregiving responsibilities. As with ADL, IADL, and behaviors, the caregiving balance will evolve as your loved one's needs and your work and family obligations change with time.

About the Authors

Laura Town

Laura Town has authored numerous publications of special interest to the aging population, including *Advance Directives, Durable Power of Attorney, Wills, and Other Legal Considerations*. She has also written for the American Medical Writers Association, and her work has been published by the American Society of Journalists and Authors. She is the former President of the Indiana chapter of the American Medical Writers Association.

Karen Kassel

Karen Kassel received her Ph.D. in Pharmacology from the Department of Pharmacology and Experimental Neurosciences at the University of Nebraska Medical Center in Omaha, where she was the recipient of an American Heart Association fellowship and several regional and national awards for her research on G protein-coupled receptor signaling in airways. She then pursued post-doctoral research projects at the University of North Carolina–Chapel Hill and the University of Kansas Medical Center, again receiving fellowships from the PhRMA Foundation and the American Heart Association, respectively. She has published research in the *American Journal of Pathology*, *Journal of Biological Chemistry*, and *Journal of Pharmacology and Experimental Therapeutics*. In addition, Karen is board-certified for editing life sciences (BELS-certified).

Rachael Mann

Rachael Mann is a writer and editor and specializes in creating educational materials. Her primary focus is on scientific and business topics. Since coming to WilliamsTown, Rachael has edited and developed materials for Pearson Education, John Wiley and Sons, and Nature Education, among others. These experiences have afforded her the opportunity to work with exceptional authors to craft informative, audience-minded texts.

A Note from the Authors

Thank you for purchasing our book! Worldwide, over 40 million people suffer from Alzheimer's disease, and that number is expected to increase significantly within the next 15 years. In the United States, five million people have the disease, and that is expected to triple by the year 2050.

Despite these large numbers, you may feel alone. I (Laura) know that when I started caring for my father, who had early-onset Alzheimer's disease, I felt alone. Although my father has passed away, I am haunted by what he suffered and how difficult it was to care for him. However, now I know that there are people, resources, and organizations that can help others going through this same struggle.

We recognize that caregivers have emotional, physical, and financial challenges. We hope that the information in the *Alzheimer's Roadmap* series will ease some of your stress. The information included in this book can help you understand the changes to ADL, IADL, and behavior your loved one may be experiencing and prepare you to provide appropriate, compassionate care and assistance. In addition, we have included resources at the end of each book to provide additional information to help you through this process.

If you have any questions for us, feel free to post them on Laura Town's Amazon Author Central page or reach out to the authors via twitter: @laurawtown, @KarenKassel1, and @RachaelLMann1. We would appreciate it if you would take the time to review our book on Amazon, as our book's visibility on Amazon depends on reviews.

More Titles from
Laura Town and Karen Kassel

Alzheimer's Roadmap series:

*Long-Term Care Insurance, Power of Attorney,
Wealth Management, and Other First Steps*

*Dementia, Alzheimer's Disease Stages, Treatment
Options, and Other Medical Considerations*

*Advance Directives, Durable Power of Attorney,
Wills, and Other Legal Considerations*

*Home Safety Checklist Guide and Caregiver Resources
for Medication Safety, Driving, and Wandering*

*Home Care, Long-Term Care, Memory Care Units,
and Other Living Arrangements*

Caregiver Resources: From Independence to a Memory Care Unit

Nutrition for Brain Health: Fighting Dementia

Paying for Healthcare and Other Financial Considerations

Resources

Information Resources:

Alzheimer's Association
225 N. Michigan Ave., Fl. 17
Chicago, IL 60601-7633
Phone: 800-272-3900
Email: info@alz.org
Website: http://www.alz.org

Alzheimer's Foundation of America
322 Eighth Ave., 7th fl.
New York, NY 10001
Phone: 866-232-8484
Website: www.alzfdn.org

Other Resources:

Administration on Aging Alzheimer's Disease Supportive Services Program
Website: http://www.aoa.acl.gov/AoA_Programs/HPW/Alz_Grants/index.aspx#new
This website offers webinars on a broad range of Alzheimer's-related topics, including information about different types of care and current research in Alzheimer's disease.

Alzheimer's Association Care Training Resources
Website: http://www.alz.org/care/alzheimers-dementia-care-training-certification.asp
This website offers a variety of free and paid online training workshops that will help you learn how to care for a loved one with Alzheimer's disease.

Caregiver Action Network Video Resource Center
Website: http://www.caregiveraction.org/resources/alzheimer-videos/
This website offers short videos of Alzheimer's disease caregivers discussing how their lives have changed since becoming a caregiver and offering real-life suggestions for providing care.

Family Caregiver Alliance National Center on Caregiving
Phone: 800-445-8106
Website: https://caregiver.org/
This website offers a state-by-state resource locator for caregivers across a broad spectrum of diseases.

Fisher Center for Alzheimer's Research Foundation Resource Locator
Website: https://www.alzinfo.org/treatment-care/resource-locator/
This website offers a ZIP-code-based resource locator that covers a wide variety of topics, agencies, and types of care specific to Alzheimer's disease.

National Institute on Aging Alzheimer's Disease Education and Referral Center (ADEAR)
Phone: 800-438-4380
Email: adear@nia.nih.gov
Website: http://www.nia.nih.gov/alzheimers/
This website connects to information specialists who answer questions about Alzheimer's disease.

Alzheimer's Roadmap series

Purchase on Amazon:

Long-Term Care Insurance, Power of Attorney, Wealth Management, and Other First Steps

Dementia, Alzheimer's Disease Stages, Treatment Options, and Other Medical Considerations

Advance Directives, Durable Power of Attorney, Wills, and Other Legal Considerations

Home Safety Checklist Guide and Caregiver Resources for Medication Safety, Driving, and Wandering

Home Care, Long-Term Care, Memory Care Units, and Other Living Arrangements

Caregiver Resources: From Independence to a Memory Care Unit

Nutrition for Brain Health: Fighting Dementia

Paying for Healthcare and Other Financial Considerations

Reference List

AARP. (2015). Preventing medication errors. Retrieved from http://www.aarp.org/relationships/caregiving-resource-center/info-08-2010/pc_preventing_medication_errors.html

Alzheimer's Association. (2015). Retrieved from https://www.alz.org/

Alzheimer's Association New York City Chapter. (2009). Retrieved from http://www.alznyc.org/

Alzheimer's Association of Queensland. (n.d.). Alzheimer's disease and psychosis. Retrieved from http://www.alzheimersonline.org/pdf/psychosis.pdf

Alzheimer's Association South Central Wisconsin Chapter, Wisconsin Alzheimer's Institute, and Wisconsin Bureau of Aging and Long Term Care Resources. (2002). Planning guide for dementia care at home: A reference tool for care managers. Retrieved from https://www.dhs.wisconsin.gov/sites/default/files/legacy/aging/dementia/Pubs/ADL.pdf

Alzheimer's Australia. (n.d.). Retrieved from https://fightdementia.org.au/

Alzheimer's Compendium. (n.d.). Sleep disturbances in Alzheimer's patients. Retrieved from http://www.alzcompend.info/?p=214

Alzheimer's Foundation of America. (2015). Retrieved from http://www.alzfdn.org/

Alzheimer's Society. (2015). Retrieved from http://www.alzheimers.org.uk/

Alzheimer's Society Toronto. (2014). What is dementia? Retrieved from http://alz.to/learn_about_dementia/what-is-dementia/

AlzOnline. (2004). Dressing: Tips, equipment, and techniques. Retrieved from http://alzonline.phhp.ufl.edu/en/reading/tet_dressing.php

American Occupational Therapy Association. (2012). Dementia and the role of occupational therapy. Retrieved from http://www.aota.org/-/media/Corporate/Files/AboutOT/Professionals/WhatIsOT/MH/Facts/Dementia.ashx

Benjamin Rose Institute on Aging. (2014). Retrieved from http://www.benrose.org/

Botek, A. M. (2015). Alzheimer's and sleep: Expert answers to six common questions. Retrieved from http://www.agingcare.com/Articles/alzheimers-and-sleep-156720.htm

Bright Focus Foundation. (2013). Everyday life with Alzheimer's disease. Retrieved from http://www.brightfocus.org/alzheimers/livingwith/everydaylife.html

Caring.com. (2015). Retrieved from https://www.caring.com/

Coste, J. K. (2015). How does the personality of someone with dementia change? Retrieved from https://www.caring.com/questions/dementia-and-personality-change

Dementia Care Notes. (2015). Helping with activities of daily living. Retrieved from http://dementia-care-notes.in/caregivers/toolkit/adl/

Dementia Guide. (2015). Retrieved from https://www.dementiaguide.com/

Dementia Today. (2015). Sandwich generation. Retrieved from http://www.dementiatoday.com/sandwich-generation/

FMLA Online. (n.d.). The Family and Medical Leave Act (FMLA). Retrieved from http://fmlaonline.com/

Healthline. (2015). The effects of sleep deprivation on the body. Retrieved from http://www.healthline.com/health/sleep-deprivation/effects-on-body

Heerema, E. (2013). Personal hygiene and grooming issues in dementia: Nine tips on how to respond to these challenges. Retrieved from http://alzheimers.about.com/od/behaviormanagement/a/Personal-Hygiene-And-Grooming-Issues-In-Dementia.htm

Huddleston, C. (2011, March). Managing your parents' money. *Kiplinger's*. Retrieved from http://www.kiplinger.com/article/retirement/T066-C000-S002-managing-your-parents-money.html

Kennard, C. (2013). Psychosis in Alzheimer's disease. Retrieved from http://www.healthcentral.com/alzheimers/c/57548/161124/psychosis-alzheimer/

———. (2014). Causes of fecal incontinence. Retrieved from http://alzheimers.about.com/od/practicalcare/a/fecal_causes.htm

Larkin, C. B. (2013). How to get an Alzheimer's patient to take a bath. Retrieved from http://www.alzheimersreadingroom.com/2011/04/how-to-get-alzheimers-patient-to-bathe.html

Mayo Clinic. (2015). Retrieved from http://www.mayoclinic.org/

Medicine Net. (2015). Alzheimer's disease patient caregiver guide. Retrieved from http://www.medicinenet.com/alzheimers_disease_patient_caregiver_guide/article.htm

Medline Plus. (2014). Pressure sores. Retrieved from http://www.nlm.nih.gov/medlineplus/pressuresores.html

Modern Senior Products. (2015). Picture care photo phone. Retrieved from http://www.modernseniorproducts.com/picture-care-photo-phone-p/fc-picphone.htm

Murphy, B. B. (2000). To diaper or not to diaper? Is that a question? Alzheimer's disease and incontinence. Retrieved from http://www.ec-online.net/Knowledge/Articles/diaper.html

National Institute on Aging Alzheimer's Disease Education and Referral Center. (2015). Retrieved from http://www.nia.nih.gov/alzheimers/

National Sleep Foundation. (n.d.). Alzheimer's disease and sleep. Retrieved from http://sleepfoundation.org/sleep-disorders-problems/alzheimers-disease-and-sleep/page/0/3

NIH Senior Health. (n.d.). Alzheimer's caregiving: After the diagnosis. Retrieved from http://nihseniorhealth.gov/alzheimerscare/

Rayner, A. V., O'Brien, J. G., & Schoenbachler, B. (2006, February 15). Behavior disorders of dementia: Recognition and treatment. *American Family Physician*. Retrieved from http://www.aafp.org/afp/2006/0215/p647.html

Rosenzweig, A. (2013). Dressing and Alzheimer's. Retrieved from http://alzheimers.about.com/od/caregiving/qt/Dressing-And-Alzheimers.htm

Roth, E. (2013). Tips for reducing sundowning. Retrieved from http://www.healthline.com/health-slideshow/dementia-sundowning#1

Russell, D., de Benedictis, T., & Saisan, J. (2015). Dementia and Alzheimer's care: Planning and preparing for the road ahead. Retrieved from http://www.helpguide.org/articles/alzheimers-dementia/dementia-and-alzheimers-care.htm

Scott, P. S. (2009). Alzheimer's phone problems: Little object, big headaches. Retrieved from https://www.caring.com/blogs/caring-currents/alzheimers-phone-problems

————. (2015). Dementia and hygiene: How to solve hygiene problems common to people with dementia. Retrieved from https://www.caring.com/articles/dementia-alzheimers-hygiene-problems

————. (2015). Five things caregivers should know about constipation and severe dementia. Retrieved from https://www.caring.com/articles/5-things-caregivers-should-know-about-constipation-and-severe-dementia

————. (2015). How to communicate better with someone who has early-stage Alzheimer's. Retrieved from https://www.caring.com/articles/how-to-communicate-with-alzheimers-patients

————. (2015). What is Alzheimer's disease: What you should know about Alzheimer's disease. Retrieved from https://www.caring.com/articles/alzheimers-disease

Shelkey, M., & Wallace, M. (2012). Katz index of independence in activities of daily living (ADL). Retrieved from http://consultgerirn.org/uploads/File/trythis/try_this_2.pdf

Smith, M., Russell, D., & White, M. (2015). Alzheimer's behavior management: Tips for managing common symptoms and problems in dementia patients. Retrieved from http://www.helpguide.org/articles/alzheimers-dementia/alzheimers-behavior-management.htm

Sollitto, M. (2015). Sundowner's syndrome. Retrieved from http://www.agingcare.com/Articles/sundowners-syndrome-133187.htm

The Hartford. (2015). Dementia and driving: The driver to passenger transition. Retrieved from http://www.thehartford.com/mature-market-excellence/when-to-stop-driving

Thomas, D., McMachon, A., & Thomas, Y. L., eds. (2014). Moving and handling people: The New Zealand guidelines 2012; section 4: Techniques for moving and handling people. Retrieved from http://www.acc.co.nz/PRD_EXT_CSMP/groups/external_ip/documents/guide/wpc108936.pdf

Udesky, L. (2015). Sundown syndrome: What to do when someone shows signs of sundown syndrome. Retrieved from https://www.caring.com/articles/sundown-syndrome

University of Maryland Medical Center. (2013). Alzheimer's disease. Retrieved from http://umm.edu/health/medical/altmed/condition/alzheimers-disease

University of Waterloo Murray Alzheimer Research and Education Program. (n.d.). Grocery shopping and buying food. Retrieved from https://uwaterloo.ca/murray-alzheimer-research-and-education-program/education-and-knowledge-translation/products-education-tools/by-us-for-us-guides/food-mealtime/grocery-shopping-buying-food

WebMD. (2015). Personal care for a loved one with Alzheimer's disease. Retrieved from http://www.webmd.com/alzheimers/guide/caring-loved-ones

BORN INTO POVERTY, SOLD INTO MARRIAGE, AND NOMINATED FOR PRESIDENT BEFORE WOMEN HAD THE RIGHT TO VOTE, VICTORIA WOODHULL WAS NEARLY ERASED FROM HISTORY.

Discover the forgotten true story of this amazing woman, who overcame an abusive childhood, a coercive marriage, and the scorn of her society to fight for equality in life and love.

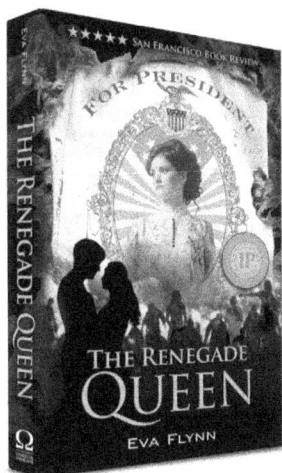

Available on Amazon.com

"Flynn hews closely to historical facts as she tells the story of Victoria Woodhull, a suffragist and reformer who worked as a fraudulent clairvoyant, opened a Wall Street brokerage with her sister, spent time in jail on obscenity charges, and ran for president in 1872. Flynn turns a history with no shortage of drama into compelling fiction, with a vivid setting and strong secondary characters, particularly Victoria's unfiltered younger sister and frequent sidekick, Tennessee. ...The woman known to the tabloids of her era as 'Mrs. Satan' is rendered as both driven and flawed, a fully realized character who will keep readers turning the pages."

—KIRKUS

"This amazingly good debut novel by Eva Flynn stars Victoria Woodhull, a figure so outrageous and improbable that most of Flynn's readers will be tempted at first to think she's an invention of the author. And yet, no! ... Flynn embarks on the story of this remarkable woman with unabashed enthusiasm, giving us her upbringing, her loves, her controversies, and the controversies that attended this figure Flynn calls a 'forgotten feminist.' Flynn's storytelling is so energetic and her characters so vividly drawn that in addition to being eye-opening on many levels ..., it is also a page-turner."

—HISTORICAL NOVEL SOCIETY

Alzheimer's Roadmap Series

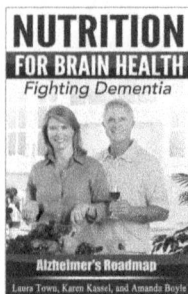

NUTRITION FOR BRAIN HEALTH
Fighting Dementia
Alzheimer's Roadmap
Laura Town, Karen Kassel, and Amanda Boyle

"A very good book with affordable foods that can make a difference in a person's brain function. My husband has the beginning signs of dementia, since we have been eating many of the suggested foods here, he has shown great improvement. A must read."

—Mary L. Whiting, Amazon reviewer

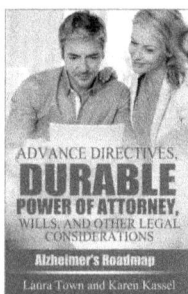

ADVANCE DIRECTIVES, DURABLE POWER OF ATTORNEY, WILLS, AND OTHER LEGAL CONSIDERATIONS
Alzheimer's Roadmap
Laura Town and Karen Kassel

"You do not need the burden of seeking out information when someone else has so painstakingly compiled the data. Even if your loved one does not have Alzheimer's disease, but you are considering placing them in a nursing facility, this ebook is incredibly helpful."

—Chris Qualls, Amazon reviewer

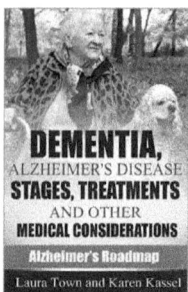

DEMENTIA, ALZHEIMER'S DISEASE STAGES, TREATMENTS AND OTHER MEDICAL CONSIDERATIONS
Alzheimer's Roadmap
Laura Town and Karen Kassel

"A great overview of the subject along with a lot of practical information. Some of the practical stuff would apply to medical issues other than Alzheimer's. I highly recommend it."

—Walt, Amazon reviewer

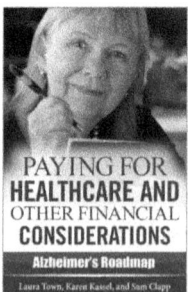

PAYING FOR HEALTHCARE AND OTHER FINANCIAL CONSIDERATIONS
Alzheimer's Roadmap
Laura Town, Karen Kassel, and Sam Clapp

"This book is amazingly detailed—not to the point where the information is repetitive, of course, but the author seems to know exactly what to include to make it comprehensive. ... If your loved one has Alzheimer's, get this book—it is of tremendous help and will save you from some unnecessary stress!"

—cc2015, Amazon reviewer

www.ingramcontent.com/pod-product-compliance
Lightning Source LLC
Chambersburg PA
CBHW032113280326
41933CB00009B/827